BIBLE WORDS CROSSWORD PUZZLES 3

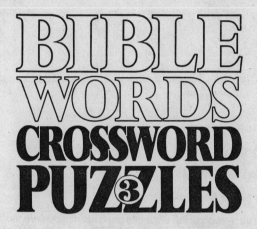

BIBLE WORDS CROSSWORD PUZZLES ③

MARVIN KANANEN

BAKER BOOK HOUSE
Grand Rapids, Michigan 49516

The fifty crossword puzzles
in this book are purposely designed
to help the users uncover Bible truths
as they solve the puzzle clues.
Most of the clues
are based on Scripture references.
Solutions are placed
at the back of the book.
Happy puzzling!

1

Across

1. Nevertheless ____ heart was perfect. (1 Kings 15:14)
5. Israel journeyed, and spread his tent beyond the tower of ____. (Gen. 35:21)
9. Sin is the transgression of the ____. (1 John 3:4)
12. Will ye ____ the souls of my people? (Ezek. 13:18)
13. Enter ye in at the strait ____. (Matt. 7:13)
14. We know not: he is of ____; ask him. (John 9:21)
15. I will put my laws ____ their mind. (Heb. 8:10)
16. Seven women will ____ hold of one man. (Isa. 4:1 GNB)
17. We ____ Jesus, who was made a little lower than the angels. (Heb. 2:9)
18. The kingdom of ____ king of Bashan. (Num. 32:33)
20. The church that is at Babylon, ____ together with you, saluteth you. (1 Peter 5:13)
22. I am the Lord, which ____ you. (Lev. 22:32)
26. The two sons of ____, Hophni and Phinehas. (1 Sam. 1:3)
27. Why make ye this ____, and weep? (Mark 5:39)
28. The ____ sitting upon the young, or upon the eggs. (Deut. 22:6)
30. The lion shall eat ____ like the bullock. (Isa. 65:25)
34. Sing unto the Lord with the ____. (Ps. 98:5)
36. If a man is lazy, the rafters ____. (Eccles. 10:18 NIV).
38. Take my ____ upon you, and learn from me. (Matt. 11:29)
39. Her sons are these; Jesher, and Shobab, and ____. (1 Chron. 2:18)
41. His sons shall put their hands upon the head of the ____. (Exod. 29:15)
43. The number of the beast: for it is the number of a ____. (Rev. 13:18)
44. They see Jesus walking on the ____. (John 6:19)
46. You have been born again as the children of a ____ who is immortal. (1 Peter 1:23 GNB)
48. In all things shewing thyself a ____ of good works. (Titus 2:7)
52. See thou ____ it not: I am thy fellowservant. (Rev. 19:10)

53. Whose soever sins ye remit, they ____ remitted unto them. (John 20:23)
54. Anyone who ____ what is good is from God. (3 John 11 NIV)
56. By faith ____ offered unto God a more excellent sacrifice. (Heb. 11:4)
60. And Philip ____ thither to him. (Acts 8:30)
61. Can the blind ____ the blind? (Luke 6:39)
62. The prayer of faith shall ____ the sick. (James 5:15)
63. Then cometh the ____, when he shall have delivered up the kingdom to God. (1 Cor. 15:24)
64. He who makes haste with his feet ____. (Prov. 19:2 NASB)
65. His own self bare our sins in his own body on the ____. (1 Peter 2:24)

Down

1. ____ the son of Abdiel, the son of Guni. (1 Chron. 5:15)
2. The city had no need of the ____. (Rev. 21:23)
3. Go to the ____, thou sluggard. (Prov. 6:6)
4. Let us set for him there a bed, and a table, and a ____. (2 Kings 4:10)
5. Is there any taste in the white of an ____? (Job 6:6)
6. For we ____ not make ourselves of the number. (2 Cor. 10:12)
7. We spend our years as _____ that is told. (Ps. 90:9)
8. I will purge out from among you the ____. (Ezek. 20:38)
9. Little children, it is the ____ time. (1 John 2:18)
10. Shammah the son of ____ the Hararite. (2 Sam. 23:11)
11. They will ____ out of his kingdom everything that causes sin. (Matt. 13:41 NIV)
19. They shall be priests of ____ and of Christ. (Rev. 20:6)
21. For he looked for a ____ which hath foundations. (Heb. 11:10)
22. He saith among the trumpets, ____ ____. (Job 39:25)
23. The twelfth month, that is, the month ____. (Esther 3:7)

24. Who shall not fear thee, O ____. (Rev. 15:4)
25. The napkin, that ____ about his head. (John 20:7)
29. Your mice that ____ the land. (1 Sam. 6:5)
31. Claudius had commanded all Jews to depart from ____. (Acts 18:2)
32. The children of Ezer are . . . Bilhan, and Zaavan, and ____. (Gen. 36:27)
33. I ____ up by revelation. (Gal. 2:2)
35. Now my days are swifter than a ____. (Job 9:25)
37. Stand in the ____ before me for the land. (Ezek. 22:30)
40. It is easier for a camel to go through the eye of a ____. (Matt. 19:24)
42. Much learning doth make thee ____. (Acts 26:24)

45. Shema, the son of Joel, who dwelt in ____. (1 Chron. 5:8)
47. Give flesh to ____ for the priest. (1 Sam. 2:15)
48. She shall shave her head, and ____ her nails. (Deut. 21:12)
49. The sons of Dishan; Uz, and ____. (1 Chron. 1:42)
50. The thoughts of the diligent ____ only to plenteousness. (Prov. 21:5)
51. Let us draw ____ with a true heart. (Heb. 10:22)
55. Hayden's 1960s political group.
57. Blessed are thou, Simon ____-jona. (Matt. 16:17)
58. Adam called his wife's name ____. (Gen. 3:20)
59. We sailed to the ____ of Crete. (Acts 27:7 NIV)

2

Across

1. And the ____, which the Lord God had taken from man. (Gen. 2:22)
4. The new ____ doth burst the bottles. (Mark 2:22)
8. House (Spanish).
12. Why make ye this ____, and weep? (Mark 5:39)
13. Simon's wife's mother lay sick of a fever, and ____ they tell him of her. (Mark 1:30)
14. Doth God take care for ____? (1 Cor. 9:9)
15. Behold I make all things ____. (Rev. 21:5)
16. Do good, and ____, hoping for nothing again. (Luke 6:35)
17. The Jews . . . took unto them certain ____ fellows of the baser sort. (Acts 17:5)
18. Ye men of ____, why stand ye gazing up into heaven? (Acts 1:11)
20. Let him ____ it as of the ability which God giveth. (1 Peter 4:11)
21. The sky is ____ and lowring. (Matt. 16:3)
22. Wherein was the golden pot that had manna, and ____ rod that budded. (Heb. 9:4)
26. The daughter of Herodias danced before them, and pleased ____. (Matt. 14:6)
29. No man hath seen God at ____ time. (1 John 4:12)
30. There were so many, yet was not the ____ broken. (John 21:11)
31. Which is to day in the field, and to morrow is cast into the ____. (Luke 12:28)
32. Tell me, ____ thou a Roman? (Acts 22:27)
33. ____ obeyed Abraham, calling him lord. (1 Peter 3:6)
34. Leguminous plant.
35. Ye know not what ye ____. (Mark 10:38)
36. To irritate.
37. They are vanity, the work of ____. (Jer. 51:18)
39. Pewter coin.
40. To supply your lack of service toward ____. (Phil. 2:30)
41. ____ ye that I am come to give peace on earth? (Luke 12:51)
45. Shammah the son of ____ the Hararite. (2 Sam. 23:11)
48. ____ said, Intreat me not to leave thee. (Ruth 1:16)
49. Gathered the good into vessels, but cast the ____ away. (Matt. 13:48)
50. When they had ____ an hymn, they went out. (Mark 14:26)
51. South American copper district.
52. The serpent beguiled ____. (2 Cor. 11:3)
53. Our ____ of activity among you will greatly expand. (2 Cor. 10:15 NIV)
54. The ____ ran violently down a steep place. (Luke 8:33)
55. Is this house . . . become a ____ of robbers in your eyes? (Jer. 7:11)

Down

1. Shout, so that the earth ____ again. (1 Sam.. 4:5)
2. Their ____ of pleasure is to carouse. (2 Peter 2:13 NIV)
3. The silver cord be loosed, or the golden ____ be broken. (Eccles. 12:6)
4. The cities are great and ____ up to heaven. (Deut. 1:28)
5. Have _____ of mad men? (1 Sam. 21:15)
6. Fear ____ of these things which thou shalt suffer. (Rev. 2:10)
7. Then cometh the ____, when he shall have delivered up the kingdom to God. (1 Cor. 15:24)
8. If the plague has not changed its ____. (Lev. 13:55 NKJV)
9. Even now the ____ is laid to the root of the trees. (Luke 3:9 RSV)
10. Woe to the women that ____ pillows. (Ezek. 13:18)
11. ____ beside this, giving all diligence, add to your faith virtue. (2 Peter 1:5)
19. Having their conscience seared with a hot ____. (1 Tim. 4:2)
20. Glorify God in the ____ of visitation. (1 Peter 2:12)
22. Go to the ____, thou sluggard. (Prov. 6:6)
23. The sons of Judah were Er and ____. (Num. 26:19)
24. When Paul was brought before ____. (2 Tim. Subs.)
25. ____ on horses, and trust in chariots. (Isa. 31:1)

8

26. And Lord Jesus Christ, which is our ____. (1 Tim. 1:1)
27. He told me all that ____ I did. (John 4:39)
28. Wilt thou ____ it up in three days? (John 2:20)
29. There was seen in his temple the ____ of his testament. (Rev. 11:19)
32. A colt the foal of an ____. (Matt. 21:5)
33. The silver chain will ____. (Eccles. 12:6 GNB)
35. Were your children unclean; but now ____ they holy? (1 Cor. 7:14)
36. Where are the gods of Hamath and ____? (Isa. 36:19)
38. I am Alpha and ____, the first and the last. (Rev. 1:11)
39. The law was our ____ to bring us to Christ. (Gal. 3:24 NKJV)
41. The foundation of God standeth ____. (2 Tim. 2:19)
42. Booz begat ____ of Ruth. (Matt. 1:5)
43. Even baptism doth also now ____ us. (1 Peter 3:21)
44. Thou hast been in ____ the garden of God. (Ezek. 28:13)
45. Maachah the mother of ____ the king. (2 Chron. 15:16)
46. They did so at the going up to ____. (2 Kings 9:27)
47. Direction: Jerusalem to Jericho.
48. College cheer.

3

Across

1. As the flower of the grass he shall ____ away. (James 1:10)
5. Deliver thyself as a ____ from the hand of the hunter. (Prov. 6:5)
8. The ____, and the pelican. (Lev. 11:18)
12. Double-reeded woodwind.
13. He touched his ____, and healed him. (Luke 22:51)
14. Casting all your ____ upon him. (1 Peter 5:7)
15. Withered.
16. To make ready a people ____ for the Lord. (Luke 1:17)
18. ____ begat Manasses. (Matt. 1:10)
20. To ____ inheritance, incorruptible, and undefiled. (1 Peter 1:4)
21. If ____ of you lack wisdom, let him ask of God. (James 1:5)
22. That ye may ____ upon the Lord without distraction. (1 Cor. 7:35)
26. Unto him that is able to do exceeding abundantly above all that we ask or ____. (Eph. 3:20)
29. Ye have an unction from the Holy ____. (1 John 2:20)
30. Hath Satan filled thine heart to ____? (Acts 5:3)
31. And thrust my ____ into his side, I will not believe. (John 20:25)
32. The lapwing, and the ____. (Lev. 11:19)
33. A ____ of him shall not be broken. (John 19:36)
34. Circle segment.
35. They ____ my path. (Job 30:13)
36. I ____ standing among them. (Acts 24:21)
37. Iranian capital.
39. Animal constellation.
40. Joshua burnt ____, and made it an heap for ever. (Josh. 8:28)
41. He saw a man, named ____, sitting at the receipt of custom. (Matt. 9:9)
45. To him be glory and ____ for ever. (1 Peter 5:11)
49. ____ us from the face of him that sitteth on the throne. (Rev. 6:16)
50. The sons of Judah were Er and ____. (Num. 26:19)
51. Even the ____ in the field deserts her newborn fawn. (Jer. 14:5 NIV)
52. He that doeth the will of God abideth for ____. (1 John 2:17)
53. The ____ of the workers of iniquity. (Ps. 141:9)
54. Being (Latin).
55. The earth did quake, and the rocks ____. (Matt. 27:51)

Down

1. Son of man, ____ a riddle, and speak a parable. (Ezek. 17:2 NIV)
2. Rabbith, and Kishion, and ____. (Josh. 19:20)
3. The spirit cried, and rent him ____. (Mark 9:26)
4. The Son of man is come to ____ ____ to save. (Luke 19:10)
5. When I come again, I will ____ thee. (Luke 10:35)
6. Of the oaks of Bashan have they made thine ____. (Ezek. 27:6)
7. ____ the lamp of God went out in the temple. (1 Sam. 3:3)
8. The ____ measure that is abominable. (Micah 6:10)
9. We do not ____ after the flesh. (2 Cor. 10:3)
10. Thou shouldest set in order the things that ____ wanting. (Titus 1:5)
11. Man's name.
17. His violent dealing shall come down upon his own ____. (Ps. 7:16)
19. I wrote them with ____ in the book. (Jer. 36:18)
22. Go to the ____, thou sluggard. (Prov. 6:6)
23. ____, lama sabachthani? (Mark 15:34)
24. Were there not ten cleansed? but where are the ____? (Luke 17:17)
25. This man shall be blessed in his ____. (James 1:25)
26. ____ the trial of your faith. (1 Peter 1:7)
27. The ____ . . . is unclean unto you. (Lev. 11:6)
28. Fraction of a foot.
29. All that handle the ____, the mariners. (Ezek. 27:29)
32. Achar, who brought disaster on Israel by violating the ____. (1 Chron. 2:7 NIV)

Crossword grid with numbered cells (1–55) and handwritten answers.

Clues

33. Whosoever hateth his ____ is a murderer. (1 John 3:15)
35. Fire spread from one of its ____ branches. (Ezek. 19:14 NIV)
36. French pronoun.
38. How patient he is for the autumn and spring ____. (James 5:7 NIV)
39. Go out quickly into the streets and ____. (Luke 14:21)
41. There is one glory of the sun, and another glory of the ____. (1 Cor. 15:41)
42. Honeybee home.

43. He will make her wilderness like ____. (Isa. 51:3)
44. Thou, being a wild olive tree, ____ graffed in. (Rom. 11:17)
45. After whom dost thou pursue? after a dead ____? (1 Sam. 24:14)
46. She called his name Ben-____; but his father called him Benjamin. (Gen. 35:18)
47. They were judged every ____ according to their works. (Rev. 20:13)
48. Chemical suffix.

4

Across

1. Blessed is he that readeth, and they that ____. (Rev. 1:3)
5. All the night make I my bed to ____. (Ps. 6:6)
9. ____, woe is unto me, if I preach not the gospel. (1 Cor. 9:16)
12. Repent: or ____ I will come unto thee. (Rev. 2:16)
13. The ____, because he cheweth the cud. (Lev. 11:6)
14. First the blade, then the ____. (Mark 4:28)
15. I charge you by the Lord that this epistle be ____ unto all the holy brethren. (1 Thess. 5:27)
16. It goes through ____ places seeking rest. (Matt. 12:43 NIV)
17. ____ begat Josaphat. (Matt. 1:8)
18. God hast punished us less than our iniquities ____. (Ezra 9:13)
20. Moses trembled and ____ not look. (Acts 7:32 NKJV)
22. The light of the body is the ____. (Luke 11:34)
23. ____, lama sabachthani? (Matt. 27:46)
24. He could not ____ to pronounce it right. (Judg. 12:6)
27. In ____ hour is thy judgment come. (Rev. 18:10)
28. Having Bethel on the west, and ____ on the east. (Gen. 12:8)
31. What things were gain to me, those I counted ____ for Christ. (Phil. 3:7)
32. Gathered the good into vessels, but cast the ____ away. (Matt. 13:48)
33. Mine age is departed, and is removed from me as a shepherd's ____. (Isa. 38:12)
34. ____, Lord: yet the dogs under the table eat. (Mark 7:28)
35. We do not ____ after the flesh. (2 Cor. 10:3)
36. And ____ rain on the just and on the unjust. (Matt. 5:45 NKJV)
37. The man got up, picked up his ____, and hurried away. (Mark 2:12 GNB)
38. Sons of Ishi were, Zoheth, and ____-zoheth. (1 Chron. 4:20)
39. If the world ____ you, you know that it hated Me before it hated you. (John 15:18 NKJV)
42. I gave ear to your ____, whilst ye searched. (Job 32:11)

46. Direction: Nazareth to the Sea of Galilee.
47. ____ the sick, cleanse the lepers. (Matt. 10:8)
49. Translucent mineral.
50. They ascended up to heaven ____ ____ cloud. (Rev. 11:12)
51. Sufficient unto the day is the ____ thereof. (Matt. 6:34)
52. J. Verne character.
53. A ____ caught in a thicket by his horns. (Gen. 22:13)
54. They wandered . . . in ____ and caves of the earth. (Heb. 11:38)
55. Past tense form of precipitation.

Down

1. The whole ____ of swine ran violently down a steep place into the sea. (Matt. 8:32)
2. Confederate General Robert ____ ____.
3. Nevertheless ____ heart was perfect. (1 Kings 15:14)
4. The Lord ____ the soul of His servants. (Ps. 34:22 NKJV)
5. In the same day shall the Lord ____ with a razor that is hired. (Isa. 7:20)
6. They were ____ of it, and fled unto Lystra. (Acts 14:6)
7. Ezbon, and Uzzi and Uzziel, and Jerimoth, and ____, five. (1 Chron. 7:7)
8. ____ not with him that flattereth with his lips. (Prov. 20:19)
9. His parents went to Jerusalem every ____. (Luke 2:41)
10. Take thine ____, eat, drink, and be merry. (Luke 12:19)
11. King ____ the Canaanite, which dwelt in the south. (Num. 21:1)
19. Barley in its place, and ____ within its area. (Isa. 28:25 NASB)
21. They fled before the men of ____. (Josh 7:4)
23. The ____ of all flesh is come before me. (Gen. 6:13)
24. Doth the hawk ____ by thy wisdom? (Job 39:26)
25. Deliver thyself as a ____ from the hunter. (Prov. 6:5)
26. Meek, and sitting upon an ____. (Matt. 21:5)
27. All that handle the ____, the mariners. (Ezek. 27:29)

28. Even as a ____ gathereth her chickens under her wings. (Matt. 23:37)
29. Grace unto you, ____ peace, be multiplied. (1 Peter 1:2)
30. That which groweth of ____ own accord of thy harvest thou shalt not reap. (Lev. 25:5)
32. And the lapwing, and the ____. (Deut. 14:18)
33. Am not I better to thee than ____ ____? (1 Sam. 1:8)
35. She hath ____ my feet with tears. (Luke 7:44)
36. He that wavereth is like a wave of the ____. (James 1:6)
37. Findeth Philip, and saith unto him, Follow ____. (John 1:43)
38. In that day shall there be upon the ____ of the horses, HOLINESS UNTO THE LORD. (Zech. 14:20)

39. This is the ____: come, let us kill him. (Luke 20:14)
40. ____, a prophetess, the daughter of Phanuel. (Luke 2:36)
41. Harness the ____ to the chariot. (Mic. 1:13 NIV)
42. The earth which drinketh in the ____ that cometh. (Heb. 6:7)
43. Men's sins are ____ beforehand. (1 Tim. 5:24)
44. His ____ is called The Word of God. (Rev. 19:13)
45. O fools, and ____ of heart to believe. (Luke 24:25)
48. The serpent beguiled ____ through his subtilty. (2 Cor. 11:3)

5

Across

1. A great shout, that the wall fell down ____. (Josh. 6:20)
5. The Valley of Siddim was full of ____ pits. (Gen. 14:10 NIV)
8. None is so fierce that ____ stir him up. (Job 41:10)
12. We will ____ upon the swift. (Isa. 30:16)
13. Ye tithe mint and ____ and all manner of herbs. (Luke 11:42)
14. She had made an ____ in a grove. (1 Kings 15:13)
15. Zanoah, and En-gannim, Tappuah, and ____. (Josh. 15:34)
16. The essence of being.
17. Melchi, which was the son of ____. (Luke 3:28)
18. I also will keep thee from the hour of ____. (Rev. 3:10)
21. Shamed, who built Ono and ____. (1 Chron. 8:12)
22. To have placed a call.
26. The Spirit, and the water, and the blood: and these three ____ in one. (1 John 5:8)
29. Eastern European country (abbrev.)
30. Them that were slain; namely, ____, and Rekem. (Num. 31:8)
31. Only he who ____ the will of my Father. (Matt. 7:21 NIV)
32. Filled pastry.
33. We, or ____ he come near, are ready to kill him. (Acts 23:15)
34. There ____ also many other things which Jesus did. (John 21:25)
35. Doctor of Law degree.
36. At the ____ of your flying arrows. (Hab. 3:11 NIV)
37. His chosen captains also are drowned in the ____ ____. (Exod. 15:4)
39. Who ____ thou that judgest another? (Rom. 14:4)
40. Holding the mystery of the faith in a pure ____. (1 Tim. 3:9)
45. Whosoever shall say to his brother, ____, shall be in danger. (Matt. 5:22)
48. In all things ye are ____ superstitious. (Acts 17:22)
49. Arabian weight.
50. Of ____, the family of the Eranites. (Num. 26:36)
51. They do alway ____ in their heart. (Heb. 3:10)
52. Danish money.
53. Till a ____ strike through his liver. (Prov. 7:23)
54. Will a young lion cry out of his ____? (Amos 3:4)
55. But where are the ____? (Luke 17:17)

Down

1. ____ not thyself because of evildoers. (Ps. 37:1)
2. Not to boast in another man's ____ of things. (2 Cor. 10:16)
3. As in ____ all die, even so in Christ shall all be made alive. (1 Cor. 15:22)
4. The most High dwelleth not in ____ made with hands. (Acts 7:48)
5. The holy city shall they ____ under foot. (Rev. 11:2)
6. Thou shalt not approach to his wife: she is thine ____. (Lev. 18:14)
7. That the ____ of men might seek after the Lord. (Acts 15:17)
8. Great is ____ of the Ephesians. (Acts 19:34)
9. Supposing to ____ affliction to my bonds. (Phil 1:16)
10. He shall rule them with a ____ of iron. (Rev. 19:15)
11. Samuel feared to show ____ the vision. (1 Sam. 3:15)
19. Upon the great ____ of their right foot. (Exod. 29:20)
20. Give us of your ____; for our lamps are gone out. (Matt. 25:8)
23. He saw ____ the son of Alphaeus. (Mark 2:14)
24. ____ so, come, Lord Jesus. (Rev. 22:20)
25. Whose waters cast up mire and ____. (Isa. 57:20)
26. This house was finished on the third day of the month ____. (Ezra 6:15)
27. If an ox ____ a man or a woman. (Exod. 21:28)
28. They smote him on the head with a ____. (Mark 15:19)
29. As many as ye shall find, ____ to the marriage. (Matt. 22:9)

14

32. I have ____, Apollos watered. (1 Cor. 3:6)
33. Maarath, and Bethanoth, and ____. (Josh. 15:59)
35. Lion constellation.
36. Hebrew pronunciation guide.
38. The ____ measure that is abominable. (Mic. 6:10)
39. Infant oak.
41. They all wept ____, and fell on Paul's neck. (Acts 20:37)
42. Salathiel, which was the son of ____. (Luke 3:27)

43. My ____ is the weakest in Manasseh. (Judg. 6:15 NIV)
44. Take thine ____, eat, drink, and be merry. (Luke 12:19)
45. And behold a great ____ dragon. (Rev. 12:3)
46. Jephunneh, and Pispah, and ____. (1 Chron. 7:38)
47. Smote them, until they came under Beth- ____. (1 Sam. 7:11)

6

Across

1. They divine a ____ unto thee. (Ezek. 21:29)
4. ____ was not deceived, but the woman. (1 Tim. 2:14)
8. Brought them unto Halah, and Habor, and ____. (1 Chron. 5:26)
12. For Christ is the ____ of the law. (Rom 10:4)
13. Eight-tenths of a bit.
14. Called his name ____. (Gen. 4:26)
15. I ____ no pleasant bread. (Dan. 10:3)
16. By this time there is a bad ____. (John 11:39 NIV)
17. To his sin he ____ rebellion. (Job 34:37 NIV)
18. The elders who direct the affairs of the church well are worthy of double ____. (1 Tim. 5:17 NIV)
20. And has not spread, it is only a ____. (Lev. 13:23 NIV)
22. They shall ____ thee with the dew of heaven. (Dan. 4:25)
24. So that it ____ seed for the sower. (Isa. 55:10 NIV)
28. You ____ out the word of the Lord. (1 Thess. 1:8)
32. The angel of the Lord appeared to Joseph in a ____. (Matt. 2:13)
33. Rudiment.
34. He spake by Joshua the son of ____. (1 Kings 16:34)
36. To strive for superiority.
37. And makes himself rich with ____. (Hab. 2:6 NASB)
40. Of the Jew first, and also to the ____. (Rom. 2:9)
43. One man's faith ____ him to eat everything. (Rom. 14:2 NIV)
45. We were bold in ____ God to speak unto you. (1 Thess. 2:2)
46. The earth did quake, and the rocks ____. (Matt. 27:51)
48. They passing by ____ came down to Troas. (Acts 16:8)
52. He maketh the storm a ____. (Ps. 107:29)
55. The slaughter of Midian at the rock of ____. (Isa. 10:26)
57. The sucking child shall play on the hole of the ____. (Isa. 11:8)

58. And drove all from the temple ____. (John 2:15 NIV)
59. They glorified him not as God, neither ____ thankful. (Rom. 1:21)
60. ____ was found with child of the Holy Ghost. (Matt. 1:18)
61. The earth shall ____ to and fro like a drunkard. (Isa. 24:20)
62. To preach the acceptable ____ of the Lord. (Luke 4:19)
63. Being justified by ____ grace, we should be made heirs. (Titus 3:7)

Down

1. The Lord make the woman that is come into thine house like Rachel and like ____. (Ruth 4:11)
2. Many deceivers are entered ____ the world. (2 John 7)
3. The land of Nod, on the east of ____. (Gen. 4:16)
4. Honored as divine.
5. Ye ____ run well; who did hinder you? (Gal. 5:7)
6. ____, which was the son of Naum. (Luke 3:25)
7. I will have ____, and not sacrifice. (Matt. 9:13)
8. He being not a forgetful ____, but a doer. (James 1:25)
9. When we love God, ____ keep his commandments. (1 John 5:2)
10. He that spareth his ____ hateth his son. (Prov. 13:24)
11. Balaam smote the ____, to turn her. (Num. 22:23)
19. Every man shall bear his ____ burden. (Gal. 6:5)
21. But God will surely come to your ____. (Gen. 50:24 NIV)
23. Ye shall have tribulation ____ days. (Rev. 2:10)
25. That my covenant might be with ____. (Mal. 2:4)
26. Lower Eire house.
27. Pintail duck.
28. Heber, which was the son of ____. (Luke 3:35)
29. Charon toll.

30. The man spake unto Ithiel, even unto Ithiel and ____. (Prov. 30:1)
31. Who ____ down deep and laid the foundation on rock. (Luke 6:48 NIV)
35. New (comb. form).
38. It was restored to ____, like the other. (Matt. 12:13 NASB)
39. Scandinavian country (abbrev.).
41. Teach us to ____ our days. (Ps. 90:12)
42. The fire shall ____ every man's work. (1 Cor. 3:13)
44. And slew a lion in a pit in a ____ day. (1 Chron. 11:22)

47. The leaves of the ____ were for the healing. (Rev. 22:2)
49. And with a golden ____ around his chest. (Rev. 1:13 NIV)
50. Lord, that thou shalt call me ____. (Hos. 2:16)
51. Ivory, and ____, and peacocks. (1 Kings 10:22)
52. Balloon basket.
53. There ____ many unruly and vain talkers. (Titus 1:10)
54. We passed to the ____ of a small island called Cauda. (Acts 27:16 NIV)
56. Historical period.

7

Across

1. And ____, because the shadow thereof is good. (Hos. 4:13)
5. We all do ____ as a leaf. (Isa. 64:6)
9. Praise our God, ____ ye his servants. (Rev. 19:5)
12. My blood is ____ drink. (John 6:55 NIV)
13. East Indian vine.
14. Do you watch when the ____ bears her fawn? (Job 39:1 NIV)
15. ____ obeyed Abraham, calling him lord. (1 Peter 3:6)
16. Places where David himself and his men were accustomed to ____. (1 Sam. 30:31 NKJV)
17. Emmet.
18. Is abundant also by many ____ unto God. (2 Cor. 9:12)
21. Sludge.
22. He was ____ as a sheep to the slaughter. (Acts 8:32)
23. And whose trust shall be a spider's ____. (Job 8:14)
26. He . . . chooseth a tree that will not ____. (Isa. 40:20)
28. Not many mighty, not many ____, are called. (1 Cor. 1:26)
32. He has brought Greeks into the temple ____. (Acts 21:28 NIV)
34. Pekod, and Shoa, and ____, and all the Assyrians. (Ezek. 23:23)
36. He found that he had ____ in the grave four days. (John 11:17)
37. For joy over it he goes and ____ all that he has. (Matt. 13:44 NKJV)
39. ____ the son of Ikkesh the Tekoite. (1 Chron. 27:9)
41. It will be fair weather: for the sky is ____. (Matt. 16:2)
42. The trees of the Lord are full of ____. (Ps. 104:16)
44. And of ____ -tob twelve thousand men. (2 Sam. 10:6)
46. Gideon built an altar . . . and called it ____. (Judg. 6:24)
53. Every ____ that loveth is born of God. (1 John 4:7)
54. ____, lama sabachthani? (Mark 15:34)
55. Evi, and Rekem, and Zur, and Hur, and ____, five kings of Midian. (Num. 31:8)
56. Shall be no more death, neither sorrow, ____ crying. (Rev. 21:4)
57. Snipe-like bird.
58. The love of money is the root of all ____. (1 Tim. 6:10)
59. Thy King cometh unto thee, meek and sitting upon an ____. (Matt. 21:5)
60. Lift up the hands which ____ down. (Heb. 12:12)
61. Whosoever shall compel thee to go a ____, go with him twain. (Matt. 5:41)

Down

1. Formerly.
2. ____ was tender eyed; but Rachel was beautiful. (Gen. 29:17)
3. Call me not Naomi, call me ____. (Ruth 1:20)
4. Took thence a stone, and ____ it, and smote the Philistine. (1 Sam. 17:49)
5. They ____ all, and followed him. (Luke 5:11)
6. Am I ____ ____, that thou comest to me? (1 Sam. 17:43)
7. Resist the ____, and he will flee from you. (James 4:7)
8. The ____ disciples went away into Galilee. (Matt. 28:16)
9. Nebuzar- ____ the captain of the guard left certain of the poor. (Jer. 52:16)
10. How ____, O Lord, holy and true, dost thou not judge and avenge our blood? (Rev. 6:10)
11. When he ____ you go, he will surely drive you out. (Exod. 11:1 NASB)
19. Hebrew measure.
20. We know that an ____ is nothing in the world. (1 Cor. 8:4)
23. Neither ____ guile found in his mouth. (1 Peter 2:22)
24. Sir, come down ____ my child die. (John 4:49)
25. Babylon is taken, ____ is confounded. (Jer. 50:2)
27. Hadadezer had wars with ____. (2 Sam. 8:10)
29. Blessed art thou, Simon ____ -jona. (Matt. 16:17)
30. It was impossible for God to ____. (Heb. 6:18)

1	2	3	4		5	6	7	8		9	10	11
12					13					14		
15					16					17		
18				19					20			
			21				22					
23	24	25		26		27		28		29	30	31
32			33		34		35		36			
37			38			39		40		41		
			42		43		44		45			
46	47	48		49					50	51	52
53			54				55				
56			57				58				
59			60				61				

31. Whose ____ is destruction, whose God is their belly. (Phil. 3:19)

33. Sodom and Egypt, where ____ our Lord was crucified. (Rev. 11:8)

35. The king ____ from the banquet of wine in his wrath. (Esther 7:7)

38. God, which ____ the upright in heart. (Ps. 7:10)

40. He planteth an ____, and the rain doth nourish it. (Isa. 44:14)

43. Dewlap.

45. To Hegai, who had charge of the ____. (Esther 2:8 NIV)

46. He said, Thou art Simon the son of ____. (John 1:42)

47. ____, which was the son of Seth. (Luke 3:38)

48. If the firstborn son be ____ that was hated. (Deut. 21:15)

49. And hath raised up an ____ of salvation for us. (Luke 1:69)

50. Matthat, which was the son of ____. (Luke 3:24)

51. Over the camels also was ____ the Ishmaelite. (1 Chron. 27:30)

52. Every ____ that openeth the womb shall be called holy to the Lord. (Luke 2:23)

8

Across

1. Bare your legs, and ____ through the streams. (Isa. 47:2 NIV)
5. The coat was without seam, woven from the ____ throughout. (John 19:23)
8. Western South American nation.
12. The wilderness of Sin, which is between ____ and Sinai. (Exod. 16:1)
13. Lusts, which ____ against the soul. (1 Peter 2:11)
14. ____ heart was perfect with the Lord all his days. (1 Kings 15:14)
15. Sibilant defect.
16. One or more time periods.
17. Satiate.
18. He said, "I will ____ your case." (Acts 24:22 NIV)
20. Unto God the Lord belong the ____ from death. (Ps. 68:20)
22. Having their conscience seared with a hot ____. (1 Tim. 4:2)
23. We shall ____ him as he is. (1 John 3:2)
24. The ____ reeds by the brooks, by the mouth of the brooks. (Isa. 19:7)
26. Understandest thou what thou ____? (Acts 8:30)
30. Take an ____, and push it through his ear lobe. (Deut. 15:17 NIV)
31. Come to my ____ when you save them. (Ps. 106:4 NIV)
32. They may adorn ____ doctrine of God our Saviour. (Titus 2:10)
33. Rachel ____ for her children. (Matt. 2:18)
36. I looked, and behold, an ____ horse. (Rev. 6:8 NASB)
38. Go to the ____, thou sluggard, consider her ways. (Prov. 6:6)
39. Polynesian icon.
40. Who is he that will ____ hands with me? (Job 17:3)
43. We did eat in Egypt freely . . . the leeks, and the ____. (Num. 11:5)
46. Where the body of Jesus had ____. (John 20:12)
47. The star, which they ____ in the east. (Matt. 2:9)
49. French foil.

50. Repent; or ____ I will come unto thee quickly. (Rev. 2:16)
51. ____ not liberty for an occasion to the flesh. (Gal. 5:13)
52. Spanish coin.
53. They will ____ out of his kingdom everything that causes sin. (Matt. 13:41 NIV)
54. Average.
55. Through faith also ____ herself received strength to conceive seed. (Heb. 11:11)

Down

1. Fuse together.
2. Whosoever loveth and maketh ____ ____. (Rev. 22:15)
3. That ____ whom Jesus loved. (John 21:7)
4. Shall be published throughout all his ____. (Esther 1:20)
5. Twixt's mate.
6. All that handle the ____, the mariners. (Ezek. 27:29)
7. His tongue loosed, and he spake, and ____ God. (Luke 1:64)
8. We have ____ from death unto life. (1 John 3:14)
9. Was not ____ Jacob's brother? (Mal. 1:2)
10. A continual allowance given him of the king, a daily ____ for every day. (2 Kings 25:30)
11. Learn to maintain good works for necessary ____. (Titus 3:14)
19. The son of Abinadab, in all the region of ____. (1 Kings 4:11)
21. The same day went Jesus out of the house, and sat by the ____ side. (Matt. 13:1)
24. The Lord that delivered me out of the ____ of the lion. (1 Sam. 17:37)
25. Stand in ____, and sin not. (Ps. 4:4)
26. To fit with masts and sails.
27. A man of ____, an eunuch of great authority. (Acts 8:27)
28. ____ shall be saved in childbearing. (1 Tim. 2:15)
29. Thy pound hath gained ____ pounds. (Luke 19:16)
31. Pays your share ____ ____.
34. I am ____ at my very heart. (Jer. 4:19)

35. Written not with ____, but with the Spirit of the living God. (2 Cor. 3:3)
36. From Shepham to Riblah, on the east side of ____. (Num. 34:11)
37. Downhill racers.
39. Those eighteen, upon whom the ____ in Siloam fell. (Luke 13:4)
40. The God of our fathers raised up Jesus, whom ye ____. (Acts 5:30)
41. They should bring them in and out by ____. (1 Chron. 9:28)

42. The dead in Christ shall ____ first. (1 Thess. 4:16)
44. Let us draw ____ with a true heart. (Heb. 10:22)
45. Send ye the lamb to the ruler of the land from ____ to the wilderness. (Isa. 16:1)
48. ____ destroyed her idol, and burnt it. (1 Kings 15:13)

9

Across

1. The same Lord ____ all is rich unto all. (Rom. 10:12)
5. Direction: Jerusalem to Hebron.
8. Shall ye not eat of them that ____ the cud. (Lev. 11:4)
12. And ____ men that die receive tithes. (Heb. 7:8)
13. Give us of your ____; for our lamps are gone out. (Matt. 25:8)
14. Joseph, which was the son of ____. (Luke 3:23)
15. Samuel hewed ____ in pieces before the Lord. (1 Sam. 15:33)
16. The fifth son of Bela.
17. He took them up in his ____, put his hands upon them, and blessed them. (Mark 10:16)
18. Go thy way, ____: for the words are closed up. (Dan. 12:9)
20. Huri, the son of ____, the son of Gilead. (1 Chron. 5:14)
22. Grudge not ____ against another. (James 5:9)
23. ____ yourselves likewise with the same mind. (1 Peter 4:1)
24. You shall utterly abhor it, for it is something ____. (Deut. 7:26 NASB)
27. I will ____ my word to perform it. (Jer. 1:12)
31. They had a great while ____ repented. (Luke 10:13)
32. Gold (Spanish).
33. He will ____ his donkey to a vine. (Gen. 49:11 NIV)
37. It became a boil breaking forth with ____ upon man. (Exod. 9:10)
40. ____ no man any thing, but to love one another. (Rom. 13:8)
41. The whole herd of swine ____ violently down . . . into the sea. (Matt. 8:32)
42. Makes amends.
45. He who ____ him forfeits his life. (Prov. 20:2 NIV)
49. Narrow roadway.
50. Plaything.
52. The children of Shem; ____, and Asshur. (Gen. 10:22)
53. Many of them also which used curious ____ brought their books together. (Acts 19:19)

54. Adam was first formed, then ____. (1 Tim. 2:13)
55. Seeing a ____ fig tree by the road. (Matt. 21:19 NASB)
56. Keep this commandment without ____, unrebukeable. (1 Tim. 6:14)
57. For the glory of God ____ lighten it. (Rev. 21:23)
58. The Jews build this house of God on its ____. (Ezra 6:7 NKJV)

Down

1. The sons of Simeon; Jemuel, and Jamin, and ____. (Exod. 6:15)
2. Lyra's brightest star.
3. Of ____, the family of the Eranites. (Num. 26:36)
4. To them which sat in the ____ and shadow of death light is sprung up. (Matt. 4:16)
5. In Sardis who have not ____ their clothes. (Rev. 3:4 NIV)
6. ____, come down ere my child die. (John 4:49)
7. I will send you ____ the prophet. (Mal. 4:5)
8. I am against your magic ____ with which you ensnare people. (Ezek. 13:20 NIV)
9. When the Philistines saw that their ____ was dead, they turned and ran. (1 Sam. 17:51 NIV)
10. Woman's name.
11. Behold, I am according to thy ____ in God's stead. (Job 33:6)
19. Direction: Jerusalem to Philadelphia.
21. Cockatoo palm.
24. The heron after her kind, and the lapwing, and the ____. (Deut. 14:18)
25. He is of ____; ask him: he shall speak for himself. (John 9:21)
26. I am ____ ashamed of the gospel of Christ. (Rom. 1:16)
28. Hadadezar had wars with ____. (2 Sam. 8:10)
29. Sea eagle.
30. French our or Latin we.
34. Ye should do that which is ____. (2 Cor. 13:7)
35. What mean these seven ____ lambs. (Gen. 21:29)
36. He ____ on the seventh day from all his work. (Gen. 2:2)

1	2	3	4		5	6	7		8	9	10	11
12					13				14			
15					16				17			
18			19			20	21					
		22				23						
24	25	26				27			28	29	30	
31									32			
33			34	35	36		37	38	39			
		40				41						
42	43	44				45			46	47	48	
49					50	51			52			
53					54				55			
56					57				58			

37. Among the bushes they ____. (Job 30:7)
38. Swedish county.
39. God spared not the ____ that sinned. (2 Peter 2:4)
42. ____ for the day! for the day of the Lord is at hand. (Joel 1:15)
43. Canvas cover.

44. It vomited Jonah ____ the dry land. (Jonah 2:10 NIV)
46. ____, lama sabachthani? (Mark 15:34)
47. To speak wildly.
48. Pintails duck.
51. Egg (comb. form.)

23

10

Across

1. ____, and Dumah, and Eshean. (Josh. 15:52)
5. ____ bare to Esau Eliphaz. (Gen. 36:4)
9. Though he hath escaped the ____. (Acts 28:4)
12. Although you wash yourself with ____. (Jer. 2:22 NIV)
13. Why did the heathen ____? (Acts 4:25)
14. The birds of the ____ have nests. (Matt 8:20)
15. Shadowbox.
16. The children of ____ of Hezekiah, ninety and eight. (Neh. 7:21)
17. ____ the son of Ikkesh the Tekoite. (1 Chron. 11:28)
18. The doors of the side chambers opened on the ____. (Ezek. 41:11 NKJV)
20. Ye have made it ____ ____ of thieves. (Matt. 21:13)
21. How long will it be ____ thou be quiet? (Jer. 47:6)
22. ____ thought she had been drunken. (1 Sam. 1:13)
24. The ____ measure that is abominable? (Mic. 6:10)
27. If Cain shall be ____ sevenfold. (Gen. 4:24)
31. All that handle the ____, the mariners. (Ezek. 27:29)
32. Direction: Jerusalem to Masada.
33. What ye hear in the ____, that preach ye. (Matt. 10:27)
34. Nets of checker work, and ____ of chain work. (1 Kings 7:17)
37. Trivial or narrow.
39. Affected shyness.
40. Babylon is taken, ____ is confounded. (Jer. 50:2)
41. She of her ____ did cast in all that she had. (Mark 12:44)
44. But the Lord took me from ____ the flock. (Amos 7:15 NIV)
48. The voice of ____ crying in the wilderness. (Luke 3:4)
49. ____ obeyed Abraham, calling him lord. (1 Peter 3:6)
51. The coast of Edom southward were Kabzeel, and ____. (Josh. 15:21)
52. Deliver thyself as a ____ from the hand of the hunter. (Prov. 6:5)
53. ____ for the day! for the day of the Lord is at hand. (Joel 1:15)
54. Arrayed him in a gorgeous ____, and sent him again to Pilate. (Luke 23:11)
55. The latter ____ is worse with them than the beginning. (2 Peter 2:20)
56. Jesus ____. (John 11:35)
57. O fools, and ____ of heart to believe all. (Luke 24:25)

Down

1. Aide's title (abbrev.).
2. Cords of vanity, and sin as it were with a cart ____. (Isa. 5:18)
3. Went up to ____, and fetched a compass to Karkaa. (Josh. 15:3)
4. They had no child, because that Elisabeth was ____. (Luke 1:7)
5. They which run in ____ ____ run all. (1 Cor. 9:24)
6. He went to the temple to give notice of the ____. (Acts 21:26 NIV)
7. Thy cousin Elisabeth, she hath also conceived a son in her old ____. (Luke 1:36)
8. The angel said unto ____, Fear not. (Luke 1:30)
9. Mary ____, My soul doth magnify the Lord. (Luke 1:46)
10. Gaelic Ireland.
11. The sons of Dishan; Uz and ____. (1 Chron. 1:42)
19. Hail, thou that ____ highly favoured. (Luke 1:28)
20. Riblah, on the east side of ____. (Num 34:11)
22. Adam called his wife's name ____. (Gen. 3:20)
23. French article.
24. Reapest that thou didst not ____. (Luke 19:21)
25. Pursued the Philistines . . . until they came under Beth-____. (1 Sam. 7:11)
26. Thou shouldest set in order the things that ____ wanting. (Titus 1:5)
27. Balaam smote the ____, to turn her. (Num. 22:23)
28. ____ thee hence, Satan, for it is written, Thou shalt worship the Lord thy God. (Matt. 4:10)
29. To him that overcometh will I give to ____ of the hidden manna. (Rev. 2:17)

30. If they do these things in a green tree, what shall be done in the ____? (Luke 23:31)
32. He does not ____ away from the sword. (Job 39:22 NIV)
35. This woman was taken in adultery, in the very ____. (John 8:4)
36. The children of Israel shall he turn ____ the Lord their God. (Luke 1:16)
37. The ____ of the scribes is in vain. (Jer. 8:8)
38. Let the ____ that rule well be counted worthy. (1 Tim. 5:17)
40. That the image of the ____ should both speak. (Rev. 13:15)
41. He ____ cursing as his garment. (Ps. 109:18 NIV)

42. He that heareth the word, and ____ with joy receiveth it. (Matt 13:20)
43. Ye ____ not that any man teach you. (1 John 2:27)
44. Let their table be made a snare, and a ____. (Rom. 11:9)
45. Is this man Coniah a despised broken ____? (Jer. 22:28)
46. Bel boweth down, ____ stoopeth. (Isa. 46:1)
47. Mightily ____ the word of God and prevailed. (Acts 19:20)
49. Having the same conflict which ye ____ in me. (Phil. 1:30)
50. Bitter beer.

11

Across

1. Thou wilt shew me the ____ of life. (Ps. 16:11)
5. Let us set for him there ____ ____. (2 Kings 4:10)
9. Noah begat Shem, ____, and Japheth. (Gen. 5:32)
12. Word of Irish exclamation.
13. To scorch.
14. Bravo!
15. When the day began to ____ away, then came the twelve. (Luke 9:12)
16. ____ is wisdom. (Rev. 13:18)
17. ____ destroyed her idol, and burnt it. (1 Kings 15:13)
18. He is the ____ of the body. (Eph. 5:23)
20. Called of God, as was ____. (Heb. 5:4)
22. Anah, and Dishon, and ____, and Dishan. (1 Chron. 1:38)
23. Pochereth of Zebaim, the children of ____. (Ezra 2:57)
24. All you men of ____ shall cross over. (Deut. 3:18 NKJV)
26. Doth the wild ____ bray when he hath grass? (Job 6:5)
27. The crow's raucous call.
30. That God would ____ unto us a door of utterance. (Col. 4:3)
31. I wrote them with ____ in the book. (Jer. 36:18)
32. Thou art Simon the son of ____. (John 1:42)
33. To marry.
34. Doth not your master ____ tribute? (Matt. 17:24)
35. When he ____ his bow, let his arrows be as if cut in pieces. (Ps. 58:7 NKJV)
36. Without ____ was not any thing made that was made. (John 1:3)
37. How could your servant, a mere dog, accomplish such a ____? (2 Kings 8:13 NIV)
38. The thief cometh not, but for to ____. (John 10:10)
41. The merchants and ____ of all kind of ware lodged without Jerusalem once or twice. (Neh. 13:20)
44. Shamed, who built Ono, and ____. (1 Chron. 8:12)
45. Even in laughter the heart may ____. (Prov. 14:13 NIV)
47. And said, _____ greatly beloved, fear not. (Dan. 10:19)
48. I marvel that ye ____ so soon removed from him. (Gal. 1:6)
49. I trampled them in my anger and ____ them down in my wrath. (Isa. 63:3 NIV)
50. When the trumpet soundeth long, they shall come ____ ____ the mount. (Exod. 19:13)
51. Out of Zebulun they that handle the ____ of the writer. (Judg. 5:14)
52. The lust of the ____, and the pride of life, is not of the Father. (1 John 2:16)
53. Then Jacob gave Esau some bread and some lentil ____. (Gen. 25:34 NIV)

Down

1. Whatsoever goeth upon his ____, among all manner of beasts. (Lev. 11:27)
2. The teachers of the law saw the wonderful things he did and the children shouting in the temple ____. (Matt. 21:15 NIV)
3. By a path his feet have not ____ before. (Isa. 41:3 NIV)
4. He marks out the ____ on the face of the waters. (Job 26:10 NIV)
5. Hezron's wife bare him ____ the father of Tekoa. (1 Chron. 2:24)
6. Jotham ran away, and fled, and went to ____. (Judg. 9:21)
7. That which ye have spoken in the ____ in closets shall be proclaimed. (Luke 12:3)
8. Diviners have seen a lie, and have told false ____. (Zech. 10:2)
9. Even to ____ hairs will I carry you. (Isa. 46:4)
10. That he who loveth God love his brother ____. (1 John 4:21)
11. Their thoughts the ____ while accusing or else excusing one another. (Rom. 2:15)
19. All that handle the ____, the mariners. (Ezek. 27:29)
21. Howl, O Hesbon, for ____ is spoiled. (Jer. 49:3)
23. Let him ____ in faith, nothing wavering. (James 1:6)
24. Shorn his head in Cenchrea: for he had a ____. (Acts 18:18)
25. Large primate.

The crossword grid with numbered cells (1-53).

26. Is ____ merry? let him sing psalms. (James 5:13)
27. We are exceedingly filled with ____. (Ps. 123:4)
28. Grace unto you, ____ peace, be multiplied. (1 Peter 1:2)
29. Moses verily ____ faithful in all his house. (Heb. 3:5)
31. ____ ____ slow of speech, and of a slow tongue. (Exod. 4:10)
32. The Lord, whose name is ____. (Exod. 34:14)
34. Whom ye delivered up, and denied him in the presence of ____. (Acts 3:13)
35. ____ boweth down, Nebo stoopeth. (Isa. 46:1)
36. ____; and he smelleth the battle afar off. (Job 39:25)

37. The one who ____ on me will live because of me. (John 6:57 NIV)
38. On the right cheek, let him ____ your left cheek too. (Matt. 5:39 GNB)
39. When the apostles Barnabas and Paul heard this, they ____ their clothes. (Acts 14:14 NKJV)
40. The children of ____ which were in Thelasar. (2 Kings 19:12)
41. A man plucked off his ____. (Ruth 4:7)
42. Gather a certain ____ every day. (Exod. 16:4)
43. Her Nazarites were purer than ____. (Lam. 4:7)
46. Ye have received the Spirit of adoption, whereby we ____, Abba, Father. (Rom. 8:15)

12

Across

1. The word preached did not profit them, not being mixed ____ faith. (Heb. 4:2)
5. Shammah the son of ____. (2 Sam. 23:11)
9. Roboam begat Abia; and Abia begat ____. (Matt. 1:7)
12. The seven lamps, they are to light the ____. (Num. 8:2 NIV)
13. Looked, and behold a flying ____. (Zech. 5:1)
14. ____ -shakeh stood and cried with a loud voice in the Jews' language. (2 Kings 18:28)
15. So that the earth ____ again. (1 Sam. 4:5)
16. It goes through ____ places seeking rest. (Luke 11:24 NIV)
17. The cries of them which have reaped ____ entered into the ears of the Lord. (James 5:4)
18. Heard what Joshua had done unto Jericho and to ____. (Josh. 9:3)
20. This is the true God, and ____ life. (1 John 5:20)
22. The next Sabbath ____ the whole city assembled. (Acts 13:44 NASB)
26. How long will it be ____ they attain to innocency? (Hos. 8:5)
27. The ____ number of them is to be redeemed. (Num. 3:48)
28. He that is unjust, ____ him be unjust still. (Rev. 22:11)
30. I beheld ____ as lightning fall from heaven. (Luke 10:18)
34. Eliphaz the son of ____ the wife of Esau. (Gen. 36:10)
36. Purge away thy dross, and take away all thy ____. (Isa. 1:25)
38. He ____ upon a cherub, and did fly. (Ps. 18:10)
39. In his own house is a prophet without ____. (Matt. 13:57 NIV)
41. The golden ____ that had manna. (Heb. 9:4)
43. The weasel, the ____, any kind of great lizard. (Lev. 11:29 NIV)
44. Honey.
46. It hath cast him into the fire, and into the ____. (Mark 9:22)
48. Wandering stars, for whom blackest darkness has been reserved ____. (Jude 13 NIV)
52. Providence's state (abbrev.).
53. Head of Benjamin's clan.

54. ____ the son of Nathan of Zobah. (2 Sam. 23:36)
56. In the first year of Darius the ____. (Dan. 11:1)
60. If ye be ____ of the Spirit, ye are not under the law. (Gal. 5:18)
61. They did bind the breastplate by his rings unto the rings of the ephod with a ____ of blue. (Exod. 39:21)
62. Reward her ____ as she rewarded you. (Rev. 18:6)
63. Direction: Cana to Capernaum.
64. The sons of Shem; ____ and Asshur. (1 Chron. 1:17)
65. God shall ____ them strong delusion, that they should believe a lie. (2 Thess. 2:11)

Down

1. In righteousness he doth judge and make ____. (Rev. 19:11)
2. ____ also the Jairite was a chief ruler. (2 Sam. 20:26)
3. When the ____ heard it, they were moved with indignation. (Matt. 20:24)
4. Abraham's son, whom ____ the Egyptian, Sarah's handmaid, bare. (Gen. 25:12)
5. Jephunneh, and Pispah, and ____. (1 Chron. 7:38)
6. If an ox ____ a man or a woman, that they die. (Exod. 21:28)
7. Did Hiel the Beth- ____ build Jericho? (1 Kings 16:34)
8. Is any sick among you? let him call for the ____. (James 5:14)
9. The sons of Dishan; Uz and ____. (1 Chron. 1:42)
10. Through faith also ____ herself received strength. (Heb. 11:11)
11. The Lord said unto Cain, Where is ____ thy brother? (Gen. 4:9)
19. Love worketh no ____ to his neighbour. (Rom. 13:10)
21. Wilt thou ____ it up in three days? (John 2:20)
22. God said unto ____, The end of all flesh is come before me. (Gen. 6:13)
23. Taro root.
24. Nebuzar- ____ the captain of the guard. (Jer. 52:16)
25. They should rest ____ for a little season. (Rev. 6:11)

29. That he may dip the ____ of his finger in water. (Luke 16:24)
31. He ____ the chains apart and broke the irons. (Mark 5:4 NIV)
32. The twelfth month, that is, the month ____. (Esther 3:7)
33. They straightway left their ____, and followed him. (Matt. 4:20)
35. That disciple took her unto his own ____. (John 19:27)
37. ____ is come salvation, and strength. (Rev. 12:10)
40. Blessed are ye, when men shall ____ you. (Matt. 5:11)
42. The Valley of Siddim was full of ____ pits. (Gen. 14:10 NIV)
45. Is it ____ for you to flog a Roman citizen? (Acts 22:25 NIV)

47. God, who at sundry ____ and in divers manner spake. (Heb. 1:1)
48. They had a ____ for the mattocks. (1 Sam. 13:21)
49. Ram the firstborn, and Bunah, and ____. (1 Chron. 2:25)
50. Thou hast caused men to ____ over our heads. (Ps. 66:12)
51. Whosoever shall say to his brother, ____, shall be in danger of the council. (Matt. 5:22)
55. Moon vehicle.
57. The serpent beguiled ____ through his subtilty. (2 Cor. 11:3)
58. Is this house . . . become a ____ of robbers in your eyes? (Jer. 7:11)
59. The ____ of all flesh is come before me. (Gen. 6:13)

29

13

Across

1. Straightway ye shall find an ____ tied, and a colt with her. (Matt. 21:2)
4. I move along slowly at the ____ of the droves. (Gen. 33:14 NIV)
8. Lest they should fall into the quicksands, strake ____, and so were driven. (Acts 27:17)
12. The weasel, the ____, any kind of great lizard. (Lev. 11:29 NIV)
13. Of ____, the family of the Eranites. (Num. 26:36)
14. Was in the ____ that is called Patmos. (Rev. 1:9)
15. The fruits of righteousness, which ____ by Jesus Christ. (Phil. 1:11)
16. Actor's part.
17. There is neither ____ nor female, for ye are all one in Christ Jesus. (Gal. 3:28)
18. Buried with him in ____ wherein also ye are risen. (Col. 2:12)
20. Blessed are they that ____ his commandments. (Rev. 22:14)
21. The hills once cultivated by the ____. (Isa. 7:25 NIV)
22. Their power was to hurt men five ____. (Rev. 9:10)
26. They never stop sinning; they seduce the unstable; they are experts in ____. (2 Peter 2:14 NIV)
29. If a man is lazy, the rafters ____. (Eccles. 10:18 NIV)
30. Tumeric.
31. The sons of Caleb . . . ; Iru, Elah, and ____. (1 Chron. 4:15)
32. He ____ the Spirit of God descending like a dove. (Matt. 3:16)
33. Now the coat was without ____. (John 19:23)
34. The ____ of violence is in their hands. (Isa. 59:6)
35. Our love made perfect, that we may have boldness in the ____ of judgment. (1 John 4:17)
36. If the righteous scarcely be saved, ____ shall the ungodly and the sinner appear? (1 Peter 4:18)
37. There ____ his substance with riotous living. (Luke 15:13)
39. The church of the firstborn, which ____ written in heaven. (Heb. 12:23)
40. Asenath the daughter of Potipherah priest of ____. (Gen. 41:45)
41. While they ____ them liberty, they themselves are the servants of corruption. (2 Peter 2:19)
45. Though your sins be as scarlet, they shall be as white as ____. (Isa. 1:18)
48. If ye ____ be risen with Christ, seek those things. (Col. 3:1)
49. God called the light ____. (Gen. 1:5)
50. Thou shalt not build it of ____ stone. (Exod. 20:25)
51. Cursed is everyone who is ____ on a tree. (Gal. 3:13 NIV)
52. The poor man had nothing, save one little ____ lamb. (2 Sam. 12:3)
53. Thy ____ and thy she goats have not cast their young. (Gen. 31:38)
54. Airport abbreviations.
55. ____ all things are of God, who hath reconciled us to himself by Jesus Christ. (2 Cor. 5:18)

Down

1. ____, and Dumah, and Eshean. (Josh. 15:52)
2. Through faith also ____ herself received strength to conceive seed. (Heb. 11:11)
3. There is but a ____ between me and death. (1 Sam. 20:3)
4. We have enjoyed a long ____ of peace. (Acts 24:2 NIV)
5. The persecution that ____ about Stephen. (Acts 11:19)
6. He maketh the storm a ____. (Ps. 107:29)
7. Direction: Gaza to Jerusalem.
8. ____ called Peter, and Andrew his brother. (Matt. 4:18)
9. ____ was wroth with the seer. (2 Chron. 16:10)
10. Love worketh no ____ to his neighbour. (Rom. 13:10)
11. We sailed to the ____ of Crete. (Acts 27:7 NIV)
19. What manner of time the Spirit of Christ which was in ____ did signify. (1 Peter 1:11)
20. Whom dost thou pursue? after a dead ____. (1 Sam. 24:14)
22. Give unto the priest the shoulder, and the two cheeks, and the ____. (Deut. 18:3)
23. On either side of the river, was there the ____ of life. (Rev. 22:2)

24. Let every man be swift to ____. (James 1:19)
25. As the ____ anointing teacheth you of all things. (1 John 2:27)
26. They ____ not the bones till the morrow. (Zeph. 3:3)
27. Whosoever shall say to his brother, ____. (Matt. 5:22)
28. This man welcomes sinners and ____ with them. (Luke 15:2 NIV)
29. The Spirit and the bride ____, Come. (Rev. 22:17)
32. Be not, as the hypocrites, of a ____ countenance. (Matt. 6:16)
33. Noah begat ____, Ham, and Japheth. (Gen. 5:32)
35. Daniel was taken up out of the ____. (Dan. 6:23)
36. It is not easily angered, it keeps no record of ____. (1 Cor. 13:5 NIV)

38. Let us go into the next ____, that I may preach. (Mark 1:38)
39. Like men condemned to die in the ____. (1 Cor. 4:9 NIV)
41. They of Persia and of Lud and of ____ were in thine army. (Ezek. 27:10)
42. Their ____ of pleasure is to carouse. (2 Peter 2:13 NIV)
43. They were stoned, they were ____ asunder. (Heb. 11:37)
44. Leah was tender ____; but Rachel was beautiful. (Gen. 29:17)
45. Was not Rahab the harlot justified by works, when ____ had received the messengers? (James 2:25)
46. Behold, I make all things ____. (Rev. 21:5)
47. "Pay back what you ____ me!" he demanded. (Matt. 18:28 NIV)
48. ____ trying of your faith worketh patience. (James 1:3)

14

Across

1. We do see Him who ____ been made for a little while lower than the angels. (Heb. 2:9 NASB)
4. Writing table.
8. Narrow strip.
12. ____ a little wine for thy stomach's sake. (1 Tim. 5:23)
13. ____, lama sabachthani? (Mark 15:34)
14. The ____ and warrior, the judge and prophet. (Isa. 3:2 NIV)
15. They cast four anchors out of ____ ____. (Acts 27:29)
17. Neither as being lords ____ God's heritage. (1 Peter 5:3)
18. One Aristarchus, a ____ of Thessalonica. (Acts 27:2)
20. Ye say, The Lord saith it; ____ I have not spoken. (Ezek. 13:7)
23. Cast in the principal wheat and appointed barley and the ____ in their place. (Isa. 28:25)
24. Mohammed's book.
25. Babylon is taken, ____ is confounded. (Jer. 50:2)
26. Ye are dead, and your life is ____ with Christ in God. (Col. 3:3)
29. Went up to ____, and fetched a compass to Karkaa. (Josh. 15:3)
30. Not clovenfooted, nor cheweth the ____, are unclean. (Lev. 11:26)
31. Ominous intent.
32. A great multitude of fishes: and their ____ brake. (Luke 5:6)
33. A ____ tongue brings angry looks. (Prov. 25:23 NIV)
34. Unto the coast of Beth-____ the nether. (Josh. 16:3)
35. My (Spanish).
36. John ____ baptized with the baptism of repentance. (Acts 19:4)
37. Resident of Corinth.
41. From the blood of righteous ____. (Matt. 23:35)
42. I have not ____ from being a pastor to follow thee. (Jer. 17:16)
46. Seeing a ____ fig tree by the road. (Matt. 21:19 NASB)
47. This (Spanish).
48. "How much do you ____ my master?" (Luke 16:5 NIV)
49. Under the whole heaven He ____ it loose. (Job 37:3 NASB)
50. South African town.
51. Were there not ____ cleansed? (Luke 17:17)

Down

1. Like a ____ made by a watchman. (Job 27:18 NIV)
2. Burn it in a wood fire on the ____ pile. (Lev. 4:12 NIV)
3. ____ then that ye walk circumspectly. (Eph. 5:15)
4. Though thou ____ me, I will not eat of thy bread. (Judg. 13:16)
5. Mine ____ shall long enjoy the work of their hands. (Isa. 65:22)
6. For he is lunatick, and ____ vexed. (Matt. 17:15)
7. The same dealt subtilly with our ____. (Acts 7:19)
8. The glory of the Lord ____ round about them. (Luke 2:9)
9. ____ made him a great feast in his own house. (Luke 5:29)
10. He . . . drove all from the temple ____. (John 2:15 NIV)
11. For he hath ____, and he will heal us. (Hos. 6:1)
16. You, however, ____ me with lies. (Job 13:4 NIV)
19. My head with ____ thou didst not anoint. (Luke 7:46)
20. Of Ezer are these; Bilhan, and Zaavan, and ____. (Gen. 36:27)
21. Mine vein.
22. I know what a cocky ____ you are. (1 Sam. 17:28 LB)
25. I counsel thee to ____ of me gold tried in the fire. (Rev. 3:18)
26. The sons of Lotan; ____ and Homam. (1 Chron. 1:39)
27. We know that an ____ is nothing in the world. (1 Cor. 8:4)
28. They know God; but in works they ____ him. (Titus 1:16)

30. In the press, and said, Who touched my ____? (Mark 5:30)
31. Sir, if thou have ____ him hence, tell me where. (John 20:15)
33. The blood of Jesus Christ his Son cleanseth us from all ____. (1 John 1:7)
34. Heat the furnace one seven times more than it was wont to be ____. (Dan. 3:19)
35. Bethany was less than two ____ from Jerusalem. (John 11:18 NIV)
36. Distant view.
37. Is any sick among you? let him ____ for the elders. (James 5:14)

38. Double reeded instrument.
39. The new maketh a ____. (Luke 5:36)
40. Sell whatsoever thou ____, and give to the poor. (Mark 10:21)
43. Be ____ moved away from the hope of the gospel. (Col. 1:23)
44. Abraham set seven ____ lambs of the flock by themselves. (Gen. 21:28)
45. The weaned child shall put his hand on the cockatrice' ____. (Isa. 11:8)

15

Across

1. Whose ____ is in his hand, and he will thoroughly purge his floor. (Luke 3:17)
4. Goliath, of Gath, whose height was six cubits and a ____. (1 Sam. 17:4)
8. But what I ____, that do I. (Rom. 7:15)
12. Thai language.
13. Frau's name.
14. Unto Enoch was born ____. (Gen. 4:18)
15. Pepper plant, Borneo.
16. Night (French).
17. It is a ____ thing that the king requireth. (Dan. 2:11)
18. Valley of Hinnom, often translated to mean "hell."
20. The beginning of his [Nimrod's] kingdom was ____. (Gen. 10:10)
21. Rise, take up thy ____, and walk. (John 5:8)
22. ____, which was the son of Noe. (Luke 3:36)
23. In ____ to your former manner of life, you lay aside the old self. (Eph. 4:22 NASB)
27. For.
30. For this ____ is mount Sinai. (Gal. 4:25)
31. Tumeric.
32. He ____ the lion apart with his bare hands. (Judg. 14:6 NIV)
33. My temptation which was in my flesh ye despised not, ____ rejected. (Gal. 4:14)
34. Showed effects of exposure.
36. He that doeth good is of ____. (3 John 11)
37. With silver, iron, ____, and lead, they traded. (Ezek. 27:12)
38. Is not ____ the Levite thy brother? (Exod. 4:14)
41. Arise, O Lord God, into thy ____ place. (2 Chron. 6:41)
45. Lump of earth.
46. Paul stood in the midst of ____ hill. (Acts 17:22)
47. We sailed to the ____ of Crete. (Acts 27:7 NIV)
48. They ____ to and fro, and stagger like a drunken man. . . . (Ps. 107:27)
49. Askew.
50. Now also the ____ is laid unto the root of the trees. (Luke 3:9)
51. My yoke is ____, and my burden is light. (Matt. 11:30)
52. Marries.
53. That which groweth of ____ own accord. (Lev. 25:5)

Down

1. Can the ____ grow without water? (Job 8:11)
2. Swiss river.
3. When once the longsuffering of God waited in the days of ____. (1 Peter 3:20)
4. God be merciful to me a ____. (Luke 18:13)
5. My flock lacks a shepherd and so has been ____. (Ezek. 34:8 NIV)
6. Were forbidden by the Holy Ghost to preach the word in ____. (Acts 16:6)
7. He is cast into a ____ by his own feet. (Job 18:8)
8. ____ the king of Tyre had furnished Solomon with cedar trees and fir trees. (1 Kings 9:11)
9. ____, and Dumah, and Eshean. (Josh. 15:52)
10. Two she bears [came] out of the wood, and ____ forty and two children. (2 Kings 2:24)
11. Noble (German).
19. Sons of Elpaal; ____, and Misham, and Shamed. (1 Chron. 8:12)
20. And for the ____ that is in the land of Assyria. (Isa. 7:18)
22. The hour cometh, yea, is now come, that ye shall be ____. (John 16:32)
23. One ____ and filled a sponge full of vinegar. (Mark 15:36)
24. Freud's self.
25. But their heart is ____ from me. (Mark 7:6)
26. Teacher's Association.
27. Offer the tenth part of a bath out of the ____. (Ezek. 45:14)
28. By grace ye ____ saved. (Eph. 2:5)
29. His eyes shall be ____ with wine. (Gen. 49:12)
32. Prepared a place for the ark of God, and pitched for it a ____. (1 Chron. 15:1)
34. They also may without the word be ____. (1 Peter 3:1)
35. It claps its hands in derision and ____ him out of his place. (Job 27:23 NIV)
36. The Lord knoweth how to deliver the ____ out of temptations. (2 Peter 2:9)

38. An half ____ of land, which a yoke of oxen might plow. (1 Sam. 14:14)
39. Athenian title.
40. Were as swift as the ____ upon the mountains. (1 Chron. 12:8)
41. For jealousy is the ____ of a man. (Prov. 6:34)
42. ____ the Ahohite. (1 Chron. 11:29)

43. We came the ____ day to Puteoli. (Acts 28:13)
44. Teamster's commands.
46. Give unto the priest the shoulder, and the two cheeks, and the ____. (Deut. 18:3)

16

Across

1. Circle segment.
4. And every ____ bands were loosed. (Acts 16:26)
8. It defiles the whole body, and ____ on fire the course of nature. (James 3:6 NKJV)
12. Czechoslovakian measure.
13. We get our bread at the ____ of our lives. (Lam. 5:9 NASB)
14. The ____ of this world, and the deceitfulness of riches, choke the word. (Matt. 13:22)
15. At ____, we were bold in our God to speak. (1 Thess. 2:2)
17. Ram the firstborn, and Bunah, and ____. (1 Chron. 2:25)
18. Make bare the ____, uncover the thigh. (Isa. 47:2)
19. Her bowels ____ upon her son, and she said, . . . give her the living child. (1 Kings 3:26)
21. ____ elders in every city, as I had appointed thee. (Titus 1:5)
24. ____ shall have great pain, and No shall be rent. (Ezek. 30:16)
25. There was ____ in heaven. (Rev. 12:7)
26. But to do good and to communicate forget ____. (Heb. 13:16)
28. Bring your ____ under the yoke of the king of Babylon. (Jer. 27:12)
32. French foil.
34. Daniel was taken up out of the ____. (Dan. 6:23)
36. Southern Scandinavian.
37. The ____ forest has been cut down. (Zech. 11:2 NIV)
39. Joshua the son of ____, the servant of the Lord. (Judg. 2:8)
41. We passed to the ____ of a small island called Cauda. (Acts 27:16 NIV)
42. Balloon basket.
44. Master, we have ____ all the night. (Luke 5:5)
46. We are in rags, we are brutally ____, we are homeless. (1 Cor. 4:11 NIV)
50. Uzzi and Uzziel, and Jerimoth, and ____. (1 Chron. 7:7)
51. Thou shalt ____ coals of fire on his head. (Rom. 12:20)
52. To present you faultless before the ____ of his glory. (Jude 24)

56. Strangers which were there spent their time in nothing ____. (Acts 17:21)
57. Roof edge.
58. Ye have respect to him that weareth the ____ clothing. (James 2:3)
59. Saul ____ David from that day and forward. (1 Sam. 18:9)
60. Sodium hydroxides.
61. Female saint (abbrev.).

Down

1. Suckling child shall play on the hole of the ____. (Isa. 11:8)
2. Stadium cheer.
3. Little ____, keep yourselves from idols. (1 John 5:21)
4. Prophecy never had its ____ in the will of man. (2 Peter 1:21 NIV)
5. For the sin offering and shall ____ its head at the front of its neck. (Lev. 5:8 NASB)
6. Stand by the way, and ____; ask him that fleeth. (Jer. 48:19)
7. Let the ____ pour down righteousness. (Isa. 45:8)
8. I am a worm and not a man, ____ by men and despised by the people. (Ps. 22:6 NIV)
9. ____ your bread there and do your prophesying there. (Amos 7:12 NIV)
10. Cursed is every one that hangeth on a ____. (Gal. 3:13)
11. God shall ____ them strong delusion. (2 Thess. 2:11)
16. Meadow.
20. Riblah, on the east side of ____. (Num. 34:11)
21. The one ____ five hundred pence, and the other fifty. (Luke 7:41)
22. He came into my room and tried to ____ me. (Gen. 39:14 GNB)
23. The land of ____, on the east of Eden. (Gen. 4:16)
27. Ye shall have ye tribulation ____ days. (Rev. 2:10)
29. Vocations.
30. Every ____ shall bow to me, and every tongue shall confess to God. (Rom. 14:11)
31. Went to make war with the remnant of her ____. (Rev. 12:17)

33. They have ____ the pollutions of the world through the knowledge of the Lord. (2 Peter 2:20)
35. I went down to the grove of ____ trees. (Song of Sol. 6:11 NIV)
38. Their word will ____ as doth a canker. (2 Tim. 2:17)
40. There were ____, thunderings, lightnings. (Rev. 8:5 NKJV)
43. The blind and the lame will ____ you. (2 Sam. 5:6 NKJV)

45. Wrath.
46. For this cause left I ____ in Crete. (Titus 1:5)
47. Because thou didst ____ on the Lord. (2 Chron. 16:8)
48. Woe to them that are at ____ in Zion. (Amos 6:1)
49. Heavy cart.
53. The serpent beguiled ____ through his subtilty. (2 Cor. 11:3)
54. Feline.
55. The light of the body is the ____. (Luke 11:34)

17

Across

1. The children of ____; Uz, and Hul, and Gether. (Gen. 10:23)
5. I took the little book out of the angel's hand, and ____ it. (Rev. 10:10)
8. "____ the night before Christmas . . ."
12. We have also a more ____ word of prophecy. (2 Peter 1:19)
13. The same day that ____ went out of Sodom it rained. (Luke 17:29)
14. He wrote also letters to ____ on the Lord God. (2 Chron. 32:17)
15. Whom all ____ and the world worshippeth. (Acts 19:27)
16. Hath come no yoke, and ____ the kine to the cart. (1 Sam. 6:7)
17. ____, which was the son of Cosam. (Luke 3:28)
18. Standing posture.
20. To ____ them that were under the law. (Gal. 4:5)
22. What ye hear in the ____, that preach upon the housetops. (Matt. 10:27)
23. ____, which was the son of Lamech. (Luke 3:36)
24. They cast four anchors out of the ____, and wished for the day. (Acts 27:29)
27. He ____ about—food for vultures. (Job 15:23 NIV)
31. Sweep.
32. See thou hurt not the ____ and the wine. (Rev. 6:6)
33. By way of.
34. That we may ____ every man perfect in Christ Jesus. (Col. 1:28)
37. The herd ran violently down a ____ place. (Mark 5:13)
39. Not as Cain, who was of that wicked ____. (1 John 3:12)
40. Now we ____ through a glass darkly. (1 Cor. 13:12)
41. Knowledge puffs up, but love ____ up. (1 Cor. 8:1 NIV)
44. To affirm as genuine.
48. Or ____ believe me for the very works' sake. (John 14:11)
49. There was no room for them in the ____. (Luke 2:7)
51. He saith among the trumpets, ____ ____. (Job 39:25)
52. He maketh the storm a ____. (Ps. 107:29)
53. The law made nothing perfect, but the bringing in of a better hope ____. (Heb. 7:19)
54. ____ learning, and never able to come to the knowledge of the truth. (2 Tim. 3:7)
55. How shall he . . . say ____ at the giving of thanks. (1 Cor. 14:16)
56. English cathedral city.
57. Communists.

Down

1. Nevertheless ____ heart was perfect with the Lord. (1 Kings 15:14)
2. The ____ of them shall be a witness against you. (James 5:3)
3. Operatic solo.
4. More nasty.
5. My covenant will I not break, nor ____ the thing. (Ps. 89:34)
6. Hadadezer had wars with ____. (2 Sam. 8:10)
7. This is the true God, and ____ life. (1 John 5:20)
8. They ____ the persons of men and vessels of brass. (Ezek. 27:13)
9. Bare your legs, and ____ through the streams. (Isa. 47:2 NIV)
10. Joshua son of Nun, who had been Moses' ____ since youth. (Num. 11:28 NIV)
11. Slight.
19. How ____ he love God whom he hath not seen? (1 John 4:20)
21. Time period.
24. He it is, to whom I shall give a ____. (John 13:26)
25. They used brick instead of stone, and ____ instead of mortar. (Gen. 11:3 NIV)
26. Sooner.
27. To ____, that God was in Christ. (2 Cor. 5:19)
28. Adam was first formed, then ____. (1 Tim. 2:13)
29. Meadow barley.
30. The trees of the Lord are full of ____. (Ps. 104:16)
32. A bear, and it raised up itself on ____ ____. (Dan. 7:5)

A crossword puzzle grid with numbered cells: 1, 2, 3, 4, 5, 6, 7, 8, 9, 10, 11, 12, 13, 14, 15, 16, 17, 18, 19, 20, 21, 22, 23, 24, 25, 26, 27, 28, 29, 30, 31, 32, 33, 34, 35, 36, 37, 38, 39, 40, 41, 42, 43, 44, 45, 46, 47, 48, 49, 50, 51, 52, 53, 54, 55, 56, 57.

35. Thou hast called as in a ____ day my terrors. (Lam. 2:22)

36. Now once in the ____ of the world hath he appeared. (Heb. 9:26)

37. ____ forth for an example, suffering the vengeance. (Jude 7)

38. He will ____ his donkey to a vine. (Gen. 49:11 NIV)

40. They saw a bay with a ____ beach. (Acts 27:39 NIV)

41. Scholarship (Spanish).

42. Sheresh; and his sons were ____ and Rakem. (1 Chron. 7:16)

43. We departed in a ship of Alexandria, which had wintered in the ____. (Acts 28:11)

45. Roof overhang.

46. They have ____ the blood of saints and prophets. (Rev. 16:6)

47. Sailors.

50. Zilch.

18

Across

1. The ostriches' wings ____ joyously. (Job 39:13 NASB)
5. The fever left her, and ____ ministered unto them. (Mark 1:31)
8. ____ things of the world, and things which are despised, hath God chosen. (1 Cor. 1:28)
12. What is a man advantaged, if he gain the whole world, and ____ himself. (Luke 9:25)
13. Smote them, until they came under Beth-____. (1 Sam. 7:11)
14. Greek's Cupid.
15. Since the days of ____ -haddon king of Assur. (Ezra 4:2)
16. Then shalt thou see clearly to cast the mote out of thy brother's ____. (Matt. 7:5)
17. Though it tarry, ____ for it; because it will surely come. (Hab. 2:3)
18. And ____ to each man his work. (Num. 4:19 NIV)
20. Place of origin.
22. Lot ____ in the gate of Sodom. (Gen. 19:1)
23. The Valley of Siddim was full of ____ pits. (Gen. 14:10 NIV)
24. Cometh down from the Father of ____. (James 1:17)
27. He ____ the battle from afar. (Job 39:25 NKJV)
31. Fifth son of Bela.
32. Bound up his wounds, pouring in ____ and wine. (Luke 10:34)
33. I am dark, because the sun has ____ me. (Song of Sol. 1:6 NKJV)
37. Egypt is like a very ____ heifer. (Jer. 46:20 NKJV)
40. The sons of Gad; . . . Ezbon, ____, and Arodi, and Areli. (Gen. 46:16)
41. To feel ill.
42. A public house.
45. To ____ them that were under the law. (Gal. 4:5)
49. Jesse, which was the son of ____. (Luke 3:32)
50. Saved the people out of . . . Egypt, afterward destroyed them that believed ____. (Jude 5)
52. I am the Lord; there is none ____. (Isa. 45:18)
53. Heber's wife took a ____ of the tent. (Judg. 4:21)
54. He must bring two male lambs and one ____ lamb a year old. (Lev. 14:10 NIV)
55. Tears.
56. Their words seemed to them as ____ tales. (Luke 24:11)
57. Behold a great ____ dragon, having seven heads. (Rev. 12:3)
58. If any one does not stumble in what he ____, he is a perfect man. (James 3:2 NASB)

Down

1. The king of Israel is come out to seek a ____. (1 Sam. 26:20)
2. For whom I have suffered the ____ of all things. (Phil. 3:8)
3. Nevertheless ____ heart was perfect. (1 Kings 15:14)
4. Though our outward man ____, yet the inward man is renewed. (2 Cor. 4:16)
5. And he ____ the battle from afar. (Job 39:25 NASB)
6. The ____ is withered away, the grass faileth. (Isa. 15:6)
7. Raises.
8. ____ ye of the leaven of the Pharisees. (Luke 12:1)
9. ____ the Canaanite, which dwelt in the south. (Num. 33:40)
10. It was planted in a good ____ by great waters. (Ezek. 17:8)
11. This (Spanish).
19. The pains of hell ____ hold upon me. (Ps. 116:3)
21. Behind him a ____ caught in a thicket by his horns. (Gen. 22:13)
24. ____ the torches and let the foxes loose (Judg. 15:5 NIV)
25. ____ the son of Ikkesh the Tekoite. (2 Sam. 23:26)
26. ____ and for a snare to the inhabitants of Jerusalem. (Isa. 8:14)
28. Then ____ chose him all the plain of Jordan. (Gen. 13:11)
29. Your lightning ____ up the world. (Ps. 77:18 NIV)
30. So a ____ tongue brings angry looks. (Prov. 25:23 NIV)

34. It is easier for a camel to go through the eye of a ____, than for a rich man to enter . . . the kingdom. (Mark 10:25)

35. Ye do ____, not knowing the scriptures. (Matt. 22:29)

36. Better is a ____ of herbs where love is. (Prov. 15:17)

37. When he also had smitten the waters, they ____. (2 Kings 2:14)

38. The wheat and the ____ were not smitten. (Exod. 9:32)

39. Suffer many things of the ____ and chief priests. (Matt. 16:21)

42. Nickname for Antoinette.

43. He shall not alter it, nor change it, a good for ____ ____. (Lev. 27:10)

44. After the second ____, the tabernacle. (Heb. 9:3)

46. A.k.a. Charles Lamb.

47. O inhabitant of Aroer, stand by the way, and ____. (Jer. 48:19)

48. But Benjamin's ____ was five times so much as any of theirs. (Gen. 43:34)

51. ____ no man any thing, but to love one another. (Rom. 13:8)

19

Across

1. The ____ is very pitiful, and of tender mercy. (James 5:11)
5. Cockatoo palm.
8. That every ____ word that men shall speak, they shall give account. (Matt. 12:36)
12. Mars (comb. form).
13. They think it strange that ye ____ not with them. (1 Peter 4:4)
14. Irish John.
15. Iron and brass to ____ the house of the Lord. (2 Chron. 24:12)
16. If he shall ask an ____, will he offer him a scorpion? (Luke 11:12)
17. Against a righteous man's house, do not ____ his dwelling place. (Prov. 24:15 NIV)
18. His own iniquities ____ the wicked man. (Prov. 5:22 NKJV)
20. Everyone who listens to the Father and ____ from him comes to me. (John 6:45 NIV)
22. Lod and ____, the valley of craftsmen. (Neh. 11:35)
23. Sir, come down ____ my child die. (John 4:49)
24. She hath no strong rod to be a ____ to rule. (Ezek. 19:14)
28. O sword, ____ to the right, then to the left. (Ezek. 21:16 NIV)
32. ____ every good piece of land with stones. (2 Kings 3:19)
33. Tin or pewter coin.
35. Brought them unto Adam to ____ what he would call them. (Gen. 2:19)
36. Hagar bare Ishmael to ____. (Gen. 16:16)
39. Sarah conceived, and bare ____ a son. (Gen. 21:2)
42. The gospel which ____ preached of me is not after man. (Gal. 1:11)
44. Jacob ____ pottage; and Esau came from the field. (Gen. 25:29)
45. Contribute.
48. Dwellings.
52. To declare.
53. Take an ____ and push it through his ear lobe. (Deut. 15:17 NIV)
55. We will ____ upon the swift. (Isa. 30:16)
56. No man was found worthy to open and to ____ the book. (Rev. 5:4)
57. In all things ye are ____ superstitious. (Acts 17:22)
58. Reward her ____ as she rewarded you. (Rev. 18:6)
59. He who makes haste with his feet ____. (Prov. 19:2 NASB)
60. ____, which was the son of Noe. (Luke 3:36)
61. A foolish man, which built his house upon the ____. (Matt. 7:26)

Down

1. Lest that which is ____ be turned out of the way. (Heb. 12:13)
2. Ram the firstborn, and Bunah, and ____. (1 Chron. 2:25)
3. The high priest ____ his clothes, saying, He hath spoken blasphemy. (Matt. 26:65)
4. The clouds ____ ____ and distil upon man. (Job 36:28)
5. They were not stopped until ____ ____ could go to Darius. (Ezra 5:5 NIV)
6. She covered him with a ____. (Judg. 4:18 NASB)
7. They that cast ____ into the brooks shall lament. (Isa. 19:8)
8. Thy name shall be called no more Jacob, but ____. (Gen. 32:28)
9. Hath translated us into the kingdom of his ____ Son. (Col. 1:13)
10. Where the body of Jesus had ____. (John 20:12)
11. The fire devoureth both the ____ of it. (Ezek. 15:4)
19. Pismire.
21. Bitter vetch.
24. Small (Scottish).
25. The fourth part of a ____ of dove's dung. (2 Kings 6:25)
26. The prophets that make my people ____. (Micah 3:5)
27. Historical period
29. He planteth an ____, and the rain doth nourish it. (Isa. 44:14)
30. Be thou planted in the ____; and it should obey you. (Luke 17:6)
31. Behind him, and touched the ____ of his garment. (Matt. 9:20)

1	2	3	4	■	5	6	7	■ 8	9	10	11
12				■ 13				■ 14			
15				■ 16				■ 17			
18			19		■ 20	21					
■		22			■ 23				■	■	■
24	25	26			■ 27	■ 28		29	30	31
32			■ 33	34		■ 35			
36		37	38	■ 39		40	41			
■		42	43	■ 44		■	■	■
45	46	47			■ 48		49	50	51
52			■ 53	54		■ 55			
56			■ 57			■ 58			
59			■ 60			■ 61			

34. O my son ____, my son, my son! (2 Sam. 18:33)
37. Honors.
38. "Get up! Pick up your ____ and walk." (John 5:8 NIV)
40. Will a man ____ God? Yet ye have robbed me. (Mal. 3:8)
41. Worships.
43. Ye love the uppermost ____ in the synagogues. (Luke 11:43)
45. None is so fierce that ____ stir him up. (Job 41:10)

46. I am jealous ____ you with godly jealousy. (2 Cor. 11:2)
47. Let us draw ____ with a true heart. (Heb. 10:22)
49. Operatic prima donna.
50. Brought down with the trees of ____ unto the nether parts of the earth. (Ezek. 31:18)
51. I am come to ____ fire on the earth. (Luke 12:49)
54. ____ unto you that laugh now! for ye shall mourn. (Luke 6:25)

43

20

Across

1. Nor did we put on a ____ to cover up greed. (1 Thess. 2:5 NIV)
5. To have landed.
9. If a man is lazy, the rafters ____. (Eccles. 10:18 NIV)
12. I saw in a vision, and I was by the river of ____. (Dan. 8:2)
13. Carbonated nut drink.
14. Ye know how that a good while ____ God made choice among us. (Acts 15:7)
15. Until the day ____, and the day star arise. (2 Peter 1:19)
16. ____ be thy name. (Luke 11:2)
18. For we are ____, when we are weak. (2 Cor. 13:9)
20. The ____ have fallen unto me in pleasant places. (Ps. 16:6)
21. Did not I see thee in the ____ with him? (John 18:26)
24. ____ boweth down, Nebo stoopeth. (Isa. 46:1)
25. Many knew him, and ran ____ thither out of all cities, and outwent them. (Mark 6:33)
26. David the king begat Solomon of ____ that had been the wife of Urias. (Matt. 1:6)
27. ____ thou not unto his words, lest he reprove thee. (Prov. 30:6)
30. Struck Jesus with the ____ of his hand. (John 18:22)
31. The prophet ____, David's seer. (2 Sam. 24:11)
32. Cut it into wires, to work it in the ____. (Exod. 39:3)
33. How long will it be ____ thou be quiet? (Jer. 47:6)
34. ____, which was the son of Noe. (Luke 3:36)
35. He departed again into a mountain himself ____. (John 6:15)
36. He ____ with the servants, and warmed himself. (Mark 14:54)
37. Reduced speed.
38. The understanding of this message will bring ____ terror. (Isa. 28:19 NIV)
41. An habitation of dragons, and a court for ____. (Isa. 34:13)
42. To day shalt thou be with me in ____. (Luke 23:43)
44. Wash yourself with ____ and use an abundance of soap. (Jer. 2:22 NIV)
48. Jephunneh, and Pispah, and ____. (1 Chron. 7:38)
49. Their ____ of pleasure is to carouse. (2 Peter 2:13 NIV)
50. The sons of Judah; Er, and ____, and Shelah. (1 Chron. 2:3)
51. Were there not ____ cleansed? (Luke 17:17)
52. A Prophet was beforetime called a ____. (1 Sam. 9:9)
53. Wrought iron and brass to ____ the house of the Lord. (2 Chron. 24:12)

Down

1. "He put ____ on my eyes," the man replied. (John 9:15 NIV)
2. According to (French).
3. Having the same conflict which ye ____ in me. (Phil. 1:30)
4. My ____ is not of this world. (John 18:36)
5. Did not ____ the son of Zerah commit a trespass. (Josh. 22:20)
6. For each one should carry his own ____. (Gal. 6:5 NIV)
7. Love worketh no ____ to his neighbour. (Rom. 13:10)
8. The people is greater and ____ than we. (Deut. 1:28)
9. They were stoned, they were ____ asunder. (Heb. 11:37)
10. Shammah the son of ____. (2 Sam. 23:11)
11. Ye are Christ's; and Christ is ____. (1 Cor. 3:23)
17. Give us of your ____; for our lamps are gone out. (Matt. 25:8)
19. ____ us consider one another to provoke unto love. (Heb. 10:24)
21. They ____ at me and say, "Aha! Aha!" (Ps. 35:21 NIV)
22. I will fetch my knowledge from ____. (Job 36:3)
23. A part to be played.
24. Aeneas, which had kept his ____ eight years. (Acts 9:33)
26. Noah begat Shem, ____, and Japheth. (Gen. 5:32)

27. The city shall be low in ____ ____ place. (Isa. 32:19)
28. Sandy hill.
29. Neither in tongue; but in ____ and in truth. (1 John 3:18)
31. ____ thee out of thy country, and from thy kindred. (Gen. 12:1)
32. The man's rod, whom I shall choose, shall ____. (Num. 17:5)
34. Thou hast a few names even in ____. (Rev. 3:4)
35. And so ____ Israel shall be saved. (Rom. 11:26)
36. The ____ gave up the dead which were in it. (Rev. 20:13)
37. Above all things, my brethren, ____ not. (James 5:12)

38. He ____ on the ground, and made clay. (John 9:6)
39. The ____, because he cheweth the cud. (Lev. 11:6)
40. Through ____, the Eranite clan. (Num. 26:36 NIV)
41. He saith also in ____, I will call them my people. (Rom. 9:25)
43. Chemical suffix.
45. Cleave unto his wife; and they shall be ____ flesh. (Gen. 2:24)
46. ____ shall be a serpent by the way. (Gen. 49:17)
47. Disallowed indeed, but chosen of God, ____ precious. (1 Peter 2:4)

45

21

Across

1. Be not, as the hypocrites, of a ____ countenance. (Matt. 6:16)
4. He wrote also letters to ____ on the Lord God. (2 Chron. 32:17)
8. On the tops of the hills may it ____. (Ps. 72:16 NIV)
12. Misham, and Shamed, who built ____ and Lod. (1 Chron. 8:12)
13. Earnest money.
14. What I ____, that do I. (Rom. 7:15)
15. I beseech thee for my son ____. (Philem. 10)
17. Learn to maintain good works for necessary ____. (Titus 3:14)
18. The ____ are the children of the wicked one. (Matt. 13:38)
19. "Thou art a God who ____." (Gen. 16:13 NASB)
21. Ye shall have tribulation ____ days. (Rev. 2:10)
23. The Lord ____ dishonest scales. (Prov. 11:1 NIV)
27. Jephunneh, and Pispah, and ____. (1 Chron. 7:38)
30. A living ____ is better than a dead lion. (Eccles. 9:4)
32. The name thereof is called ____ unto this day. (Ezek. 20:29)
33. How ____ she hath glorified herself, and lived deliciously. (Rev. 18:7)
35. Thou shalt in any wise let the ____ go. (Deut. 22:7)
37. When Paul was brought before ____. (2 Tim. Subscript)
38. ____ the father of Tekoa had two wives. (1 Chron. 4:5)
40. Disgusted exclamation.
42. Put on the ____ man, which after God is created. (Eph. 4:24)
43. The Lamb of God which taketh away ____ of the world. (John 1:29)
45. Until the day that ____ entered into the ark. (Luke 17:27)
47. They compassed me about like ____. (Ps. 118:12)
49. I ____ unto you with many tears. (2 Cor. 2:4)
53. ____, Father, all things are possible unto thee. (Mark 14:36)

56. Unto ____ our dearly beloved, and fellow-labourer. (Philem. 1)
58. The Lord give thee seed of this woman for the ____ which is lent to the Lord. (1 Sam. 2:20)
59. Prime ____.
60. We should live soberly, righteously, ____ godly. (Titus 2:12)
61. To keep back part of the price of the ____. (Acts 5:3)
62. Friend, ____ me three loaves. (Luke 11:5)
63. Thing (Latin).

Down

1. Their appearance is blacker than ____. (Lam. 4:8 NASB)
2. ____, a prophetess, the daughter of Phanuel. (Luke 2:36)
3. Not a forgetful hearer, but a ____ of the work. (James 1:25)
4. The seed of David was ____ from the dead. (2 Tim. 2:8)
5. ____ yourselves likewise with the same mind. (1 Peter 4:1)
6. Odyssey beggar.
7. Fair havens; night whereunto was the city of ____. (Acts 27:8)
8. When I saw, that I was at ____ in the palace. (Dan. 8:2)
9. I ____ in the Spirit on the Lord's day. (Rev. 1:10)
10. I ____ no pleasant bread. (Dan. 10:3)
11. ____ verily, their sound went into all the earth. (Rom. 10:18)
16. ____ your affection on things above. (Col. 3:2)
20. Their lives ____ away in their mothers' arms. (Lam. 2:12 NIV)
22. Went out from the presence of the Lord, and dwelt in the land of ____. (Gen. 4:16)
24. At the junction of the two roads, to seek an ____: He will cast lots with arrows. (Ezek. 21:21 NIV)
25. It is a ____ thing that the king requireth. (Dan. 2:11)
26. "Come, I will ____ you the bride." (Rev. 21:9 NIV)
27. A paralytic, lying on ____ ____. (Matt. 9:2 NIV)
28. Can the ____ grow up without mire? (Job 8:11)

29. Even in laughter the heart may ____. (Prov. 14:13 NIV)
31. Stand in the ____ before me for the land. (Ezek. 22:30)
34. For I have espoused you to one ____. (2 Cor. 11:2)
36. Let us make ____ in our image. (Gen. 1:26)
39. The wheat and the ____ were not smitten. (Exod. 9:32)
41. They have not cried unto me with their heart, when they ____ upon their beds. (Hos. 7:14)
44. Himalayan country.
46. How long will it be ____ they believe. (Num. 14:11)

48. Loose thy ____ from off thy foot. (Josh. 5:15)
50. The sons of Eliphaz; Teman, and ____. (1 Chron. 1:36)
51. How I wish I could be with you now and change my ____. (Gal. 4:20 NIV)
52. All the ____ of the earth shall see the salvation. (Isa. 52:10)
53. Praise our God, ____ ye his servants. (Rev. 19:5)
54. Large snake.
55. Achar, who brought disaster on Israel by violating the ____. (1 Chron. 2:7 NIV)
57. Set him on his own beast, and brought him to an ____. (Luke 10:34)

22

Across

1. The fourth part of a ____ of dove's dung. (2 Kings 6:25)
4. Turkish officer.
8. Who told thee that thou ____ naked? (Gen. 3:11)
12. Cornelius said, Four days ____ I was fasting. (Acts 10:30)
13. Let their table be made a snare, and a ____. (Rom. 11:9)
14. The sons of Asher; Jimnah, and Ishuah, and ____. (Gen. 46:17)
15. Sea (French).
16. Command.
17. All the depths of the ____ will dry up. (Zech. 10:11 NIV)
18. He that feareth is not made ____ in love. (1 John 4:18)
20. Jesus, who is called Justus, also ____ greetings. (Col. 4:11 NIV)
21. Wine (comb. form).
22. They smote him under the fifth ____. (2 Sam. 4:6)
23. They shall be filled like ____. (Zech. 9:15)
25. Them also which used ____ arts brought their books. (Acts 19:19)
29. Pitcher Hershizer.
30. ____ shall judge his people, as one of the tribes. (Gen. 49:16)
31. Swiss wind.
32. Bitter suffering; her ____ will swell and her thigh waste away. (Num. 5:27 NIV)
34. They took the head of Ish-bosheth, and buried it in the sepulchre of ____. (2 Sam. 4:12)
35. Blind, or broken, or maimed, or having a ____. (Lev. 22:22)
36. Waste allowance.
37. If thou ____, thou bearest not the root. (Rom. 11:18)
40. I will send serpents, cockatrices, among you, which will not be ____. (Jer. 8:17)
43. Exclamation of pain.
44. Say unto them which ____ it with untempered morter. (Ezek. 13:11)
45. Adam called his wife's name ____. (Gen. 3:20)
46. Saith the Lord, that thou shalt call me ____. (Hos. 2:16)
47. Say ye unto your brethren, ____. (Hos. 2:1)
48. By a ____ and living way, which he hath consecrated. (Heb. 10:20)
49. There is but a ____ between me and death. (1 Sam. 20:3)
50. Namely, Evi, and Rekem, and Zur, and Hur, and ____. (Num. 31:8)
51. But ____ the spirits whether they are of God. (1 John 4:1)

Down

1. Compassed the ____ of the saints about. (Rev. 20:9)
2. *A Death in the Family* author.
3. They ____ of the Egyptians jewels of silver. (Exod. 12:35)
4. We thought it good to be left at ____ alone. (1 Thess. 3:1)
5. El ____, Cretan born Spanish painter.
6. If thou marry, thou ____ not sinned. (1 Cor. 7:28)
7. Given to hospitality, ____ to teach. (1 Tim. 3:2)
8. Behold a gluttonous man, and a ____. (Luke 7:34)
9. There is ____ ____ not unto death. (1 John 5:17)
10. Estonian measure.
11. I led them with cords of human kindness, with ____ of love. (Hos. 11:4 NIV)
19. If we walk in the light, as he is in the light, we have ____ one with another. (1 John 1:7)
20. ____, didst not thou sow good seed in thy field? (Matt. 13:27)
22. Ye did ____ well; who did hinder you? (Gal. 5:7)
23. Feathery scarf.
24. Heavenly sphere.
25. ____ faith save him? (James 2:14)
26. Brought an alabaster box of ____. (Luke 7:37)
27. Who by reason of ____ have their senses exercised to discern both good and evil. (Heb. 5:14)
28. Italian gentleman.
30. Daniel was taken up out of the ____. (Dan. 6:23)

1	2	3			4	5	6	7		8	9	10	11
12					13					14			
15					16					17			
18			19						20				
		21					22						
23	24					25				26	27	28	
29					30				31				
32			33				34						
		35				36							
37	38	39			40					41	42		
43				44					45				
46				47					48				
49				50					51				

33. Jesus ____ them, saying, All hail. (Matt. 28:9)
34. This Agar is mount Sinai in ____. (Gal. 4:25)
36. Upon the ____ of their right hand, and upon the great toe. (Exod. 29:20)
37. Wood (French).
38. Evict.
39. Even in laughter the heart may ____. (Prov. 14:13 NIV)
40. The free gift ____ upon all men unto justification. (Rom. 5:18)
41. ____ learning, and never able to come to the knowledge of the truth. (2 Tim. 3:7)
42. Covered by night's moisture.
44. American patriotic group.

49

23

Across

1. Children of ____: Uz, and Hul, and Gether. (Gen. 10:23)
5. Enthusiasm.
9. Have not ____ faith of our Lord Jesus Christ. (James 2:1)
12. Do not believe them, although they may say ____ things to you. (Jer. 12:6 NASB)
13. Seeing a ____ fig tree by the road. (Matt. 21:19 NASB)
14. Aaron thy brother died in mount ____. (Deut. 32:50)
15. Great is Diana of the ____. (Acts 19:28)
17. Poor man had nothing, save one little ____ lamb. (2 Sam. 12:3)
18. The thieves also, which were crucified with him, cast the same in his ____. (Matt. 27:44)
19. I will shew thee that which is ____ in the scripture of truth. (Dan. 10:21)
21. If we say that we have no ____, we deceive ourselves. (1 John 1:8)
23. My soul ____ for you in the night. (Isa. 26:9 NIV)
26. This people honoureth me with their lips, but their heart is ____ from me. (Mark 7:6)
29. The fining ____ is for silver. (Prov. 17:3)
31. To sag.
32. In the morning it flourishes, and sprouts ____. (Ps. 90:6 NASB)
34. If they do these things in a green tree, what shall be done in the ____? (Luke 23:31)
36. By faith Isaac blessed Jacob and ____. (Heb. 11:20)
37. When she saw Isaac, she lighted off the ____. (Gen. 24:64)
39. Bow wood.
41. I gave her space to repent of her fornication; and ____ repented not. (Rev. 2:21)
42. By faith they passed through ____ ____ sea as by dry land. (Heb. 11:29)
44. Because thou saidest, ____, against my sanctuary. (Ezek. 25:3)
46. Having two horns are the kings of ____ and Persia. (Dan. 8:20)
48. Thy ____, which thou begettest after them, shall be thine. (Gen. 48:6)
52. Whose trust shall be a spider's ____. (Job 8:14)
54. O foolish ____, who hath bewitched you? (Gal. 3:1)
56. In whom ____ hid all the treasures of wisdom. (Col. 2:3)
57. Ahira the son of ____. (Num. 10:27)
58. The lips of an adulteress ____ honey. (Prov. 5:3 NIV)
59. Saying, ____, we would see Jesus. (John 12:21)
60. Impertinence.
61. My yoke is ____, and my burden is light. (Matt. 11:30)

Down

1. Saw Simon and Andrew his brother casting ____ into the sea. (Mark 1:16)
2. Reap; for the harvest of the earth is ____. (Rev. 14:15)
3. Even in laughter the heart may ____. (Prov. 14:13 NIV)
4. The accused ____ his accusers face to face. (Acts 25:16 NASB)
5. ____ said unto her, How long wilt thou be drunken? (1 Sam. 1:14)
6. Every creditor shall cancel the ____ he has made to his fellow Israelite. (Deut. 15:2 NIV)
7. Pester.
8. All the birds of the air ____ in its boughs. (Ezek. 31:6 NIV)
9. They are but ____ of silver. (Ezek. 22:18 NIV)
10. Consider the lilies of the field, ____ they grow. (Matt. 6:28)
11. How long will it be ____ ye make an end of words? (Job 18:2)
16. The other disciples came in a little ____. (John 21:8)
20. Hearing organ (Old English).
22. Dwelt in the land of ____, on the east of Eden. (Gen. 4:16)
24. God waited in the days of ____. (1 Peter 3:20)
25. Neither cold nor hot, I will ____ thee out. (Rev. 3:16)
26. Realizing the ____ that law is not made for a righteous man. (1 Tim. 1:9 NASB)
27. This was that ____ that found the mules. (Gen. 36:24)

28. ____ Lot's wife. (Luke 17:32)
30. To ____ them that dwell upon the earth. (Rev. 3:10)
33. Them who through fear of death ____ all their lifetime subject to bondage. (Heb. 2:15)
35. I therein do rejoice, ____, and will rejoice. (Phil. 1:18)
38. And the borders were between the ____. (1 Kings 7:28)
40. Save to wash his feet, but is clean every ____. (John 13:10)
43. Demetrius, a silversmith, which made silver shrines for ____. (Acts 19:24)
45. Wherefore laying ____ all malice, and all guile. (1 Peter 2:1)
47. ____, my daughter! thou hast brought me very low. (Judg. 11:35)
49. ____ obeyed Abraham, calling him lord. (1 Peter 3:6)
50. "Les Etats ____."
51. Stand by the way, and ____; ask him that fleeth. (Jer. 48:19)
52. Straightway forgetteth what manner of man he ____. (James 1:24)
53. Assam silkworm.
55. Town near Liege.

24

Across

1. ____ was tender eyed; but Rachel was beautiful. (Gen. 29:17)
5. With his own blood, suffered without the ____. (Heb. 13:12)
9. He ____ captivity captive. (Eph. 4:8)
12. The churches of ____ salute you. (1 Cor. 16:19)
13. He spoke these words while teaching in the temple ____. (John 8:20 NIV)
14. ____ hospitality one to another without grudging. (1 Peter 4:9)
15. Doctrines.
16. The magistrates ____ off their clothes. (Acts 16:22)
17. Understanding.
18. The birds of the air ____ in its boughs. (Ezek. 31:6 NIV)
20. Seal not the sayings of the prophecy of this book: for the ____ is at hand. (Rev. 22:10)
22. How long will it be ____ they attain to innocency? (Hos. 8:5)
23. The ice, and wherein the ____ ____ hid. (Job 6:16)
26. Lady's nickname.
29. I wrote them with ____ in the book. (Jer. 36:18)
31. Slope.
32. The top of the doorway was a pointed ____. (1 Kings 6:31 GNB)
34. Arphaxad, which was the son of ____. (Luke 3:36)
36. ____ Stanley Gardner, American writer.
37. He shall reign over the house of ____ for ever. (Luke 1:33)
39. ____, Lord: yet the dogs under the table eat. (Mark 7:28)
41. They might be judged according to ____ in the flesh, but live according to God. (1 Peter 4:6)
42. We can turn the whole ____. (James 3:3 NIV)
44. ____ shall have great pain. (Ezek. 30:16)
46. In works they ____ him, being abominable. (Titus 1:16)
47. His hands were ____ until the going down of the sun. (Exod. 17:12)
51. He cometh with clouds; and every ____ shall see him. (Rev. 1:7)
53. He had no ____ that what the angel was doing was really happening. (Acts 12:9 NIV)
55. Consumption and the burning ____. (Lev. 26:16)
56. Maimed, or having a ____, or scurvy, (Lev. 22:22)
57. I will ____ with the spirit. (1 Cor. 14:15)
58. The earth shall ____ to and fro like a drunkard. (Isa. 24:20)
59. I have meat to ____ that ye know not of. (John 4:32)
60. Lode angle.
61. Jacob said, ____ me this day thy birthright. (Gen. 25:31)

Down

1. He had ____ in the grave four days already. (John 11:17)
2. To be (Latin).
3. When he ____ his arrows, let them be as headless. (Ps. 58:7 NASB)
4. Zacchaeus, make ____, and come down. (Luke 19:5)
5. Thou that dwellest in the ____. (Song of Sol. 8:13)
6. The heavens ____ the works of thine hands. (Heb. 1:10)
7. He shall dwell in the ____ of Shem. (Gen. 9:27)
8. The Son of man is come ____ and drinking. (Luke 7:34)
9. Thou art ____, and neither cold nor hot. (Rev. 3:16)
10. Direction: Jerusalem to Bethany.
11. Ye have made it a ____ of thieves. (Mark 11:17)
19. Of ____, the family of the Erites. (Num. 26:16)
21. Lovers of pleasures ____ than lovers of God. (2 Tim. 3:4)
24. Their words seemed to them as ____ tales. (Luke 24:11)
25. He that doeth evil hath not ____ God. (3 John 11)
26. Mexican peninsula.
27. Of ____, the family of the Eranites. (Num. 26:36)
28. It is an ____, he is not clean. (1 Sam. 20:26 NASB)

30. He that is true, he that hath the ____ of David. (Rev. 3:7)

33. Learn first to shew piety at ____. (1 Tim. 5:4)

35. This is the ____ that ye heard from the beginning. (1 John 3:11)

38. I will ____ the names of the idols. (Zech. 13:2 NIV)

40. To him that overcometh will I grant to ____ with me. (Rev. 3:21)

43. A certain woman named ____, a seller of purple. (Acts 16:14)

45. Closes with.

48. Shammah the son of ____. (2 Sam. 23:11)

49. Two-man combat.

50. They shall ____ as lions' whelps. (Jer. 51:38)

51. Abraham set seven ____ lambs of the flock by themselves. (Gen. 21:28)

52. ____, saith the Spirit, that they may rest from their labours. (Rev. 14:13)

54. Whose ____ is destruction, whose God is their belly. (Phil. 3:19)

25

Across

1. Thick slice.
5. From Aroer on the ____ of the Arnon Gorge. (Deut. 2:36 NIV)
8. They ____ past like boats of papyrus. (Job 9:26 NIV)
12. Pentateuch.
13. Sir, come down, ____ my child die. (John 4:49)
14. ____, a prophetess, the daughter of Phanuel. (Luke 2:36)
15. Mount Sinai, which gendereth to bondage, which is ____. (Gal. 4:24)
16. Then it shall be seven days under the ____. (Lev. 22:27)
17. Viaud's pen name.
18. As many as I love, I ____ and chasten. (Rev. 3:19)
20. Though they be hid from my sight in the ____ of the sea. (Amos 9:3)
22. Sheep disease.
23. He must bring two male lambs and one ____ lamb a year old. (Lev. 14:10 NIV)
24. ____ the youngest son of Jerubbaal was left. (Judg. 9:5)
27. Who can prove me false and ____ my words to nothing? (Job 24:25 NIV)
31. Lod and ____, the valley of craftsmen. (Neh. 11:35)
32. Let no man ____ when he is tempted, I am tempted of God. (James 1:13)
33. ____ lest any man spoil you through philosophy. (Col. 2:8)
37. To hinder.
40. By works ____ faith made perfect. (James 2:22)
41. They have no rest day ____ night. (Rev. 14:11)
42. They shall minister unto it, and shall ____ round about the tabernacle. (Num. 1:50)
45. One of the rulers of the synagogue, ____ by name. (Mark 5:22)
49. Samuel said unto the ____, Bring the portion. (1 Sam. 9:23)
50. The sons of Caleb the son of Jephunneh; ____, Elah and Naam. (1 Chron. 4:15)
52. Give diligence to make your calling and election ____. (2 Peter 1:10)
53. That disciple took her unto his own ____. (John 19:27)
54. That which ye have spoken in the ____ in closets shall be proclaimed upon the housetops. (Luke 12:3)
55. Norse name.
56. Take heed that ye despise not one of these little ____. (Matt. 18:10)
57. Dairymaid (Scottish).
58. Never (Poetic).

Down

1. There shall come a ____ out of Jacob. (Num. 24:17)
2. Theatre section.
3. ____, and Dumah, and Eshean. (Josh. 15:52)
4. To take ____ the scribe and Jeremiah the prophet: but the Lord hid them. (Jer. 36:26)
5. God will ____ my soul from the power of the grave. (Ps. 49:15)
6. ____ the son of Ikkesh the Tekoite. (1 Chron. 27:9)
7. The tongue is a little ____. (James 3:5)
8. Every one shall be ____ with fire. (Mark 9:49)
9. Nautical mile.
10. God sent his only begotten Son ____ the world. (1 John 4:9)
11. To mutilate.
19. Pekod, and Shoa, and ____, and all the Assyrians. (Ezek. 23:23)
21. "Pay back what you ____ me!" he demanded. (Matt. 18:28 NIV)
24. Ye have heard of the patience of ____. (James 5:11)
25. Greet ye ____ another with a kiss of charity. (1 Peter 5:14)
26. He brake the withs, as a thread of ____ is broken. (Judg. 16:9)
28. ____ a little wine for thy stomach's sake. (1 Tim. 5:23)
29. Non-gentleman.
30. The light of the body is the ____. (Luke 11:34)
34. As a dream when one ____. (Ps. 73:20 NIV)
35. Elihu the son of Barachel the Buzite, of the kindred of ____. (Job 32:2)
36. To bring them forth of the land of Egypt into a land that I had ____ for them. (Ezek. 20:6)

37. Your wound is incurable, your ____ beyond healing. (Jer. 30:12 NIV)
38. Extinct bird.
39. I was in ____, and ye came unto me. (Matt. 25:36)
42. Their calls will ____ through the windows. (Zeph. 2:14 NIV)
43. I will cause the sun to go down at ____. (Amos 8:9)

44. After that faith is ____, we are no longer under a schoolmaster. (Gal. 3:25)
46. He shall have put down all ____ and all authority and power. (1 Cor. 15:24)
47. The Pharisees began to ____ him vehemently. (Luke 11:53)
48. To char.
51. Scottish sailyard.

26

1. ____, who shall live when God doeth this! (Num. 24:23)
5. Have they not ____? have they not divided the prey? (Judg. 5:30)
9. The heron after her kind, and the lapwing, and the ____. (Lev. 11:19)
12. He that dippeth his hand with me in the ____. (Matt. 26:23)
13. Our ____ of activity among you will greatly expand. (2 Cor. 10:15 NIV)
14. Strong meat belongeth to them that are of full ____. (Heb. 5:14)
15. Chances.
18. And to ____ for his Son from heaven. (1 Thess. 1:10)
19. A distinction in the ____? (1 Cor. 14:7 NIV)
20. ____ to each man his work. (Num. 4:19 NIV)
23. I took the little book out of the angel's hand, and ____ it up. (Rev. 10:10)
24. Among whom ye ____ as lights in the world. (Phil. 2:15)
25. Whereby we ____, Abba, Father. (Rom. 8:15)
26. It may be the Lord thy God will hear all the words of ____ -Shakeh. (2 Kings 19:4)
29. Ping's pal.
30. The pains of hell ____ hold upon me. (Ps. 116:3)
31. Diminish.
32. If the man is lazy, the rafters ____. (Eccles. 10:18 NIV)
33. The son of Abinadab, in all the region of ____. (1 Kings 4:11)
34. Brick for stone, and ____ had they for morter. (Gen. 11:3)
35. The ____ is turned to his own vomit. (2 Peter 2:22)
36. This observance will be a reminder, like something ____ ____ your hand. (Exod. 13:9 GNB)
37. ____ with thine adversary quickly. (Matt. 5:25)
40. Them . . . which used curious ____ brought their books . . . and burned them. (Acts 19:19)
41. Sin is the ____ of the law. (1 John 3:4)
46. To him that overcometh will I give to ____ of the hidden manna. (Rev. 2:17)
47. His ____ is called The Word of God. (Rev. 19:13)

48. Sea eagle.
49. Barley in its place, and ____ within its area. (Isa. 28:25 NASB)
50. He will surely violently turn and ____ thee like a ball into a large country. (Isa. 22:18)
51. There was a continual ____ given him of the king of Babylon. (Jer. 52:34)

1. Why make ye this ____, and weep? (Mark 5:39)
2. The ____ of truth shall be established for ever. (Prov. 12:19)
3. The . . . child shall play on the hole of the ____. (Isa. 11:8)
4. Bear much fruit, ____ yourselves to be my disciples. (John 15:8 NIV)
5. Your braided hair shines like the finest ____. (Song of Sol. 7:5 GNB)
6. Danube tributary.
7. Yet (Poetic).
8. His life abhorreth bread, and his soul ____ meat. (Job 33:20)
9. Does a bird fall into a trap on the ground when there is no ____ in it? (Amos 3:5 NASB)
10. *African Queen* scriptwriter.
11. Hardy heroine.
16. Jealousy is the ____ of a man. (Prov. 6:34)
17. Upon the great ____ of their right foot. (Exod. 29:20)
20. He shall suck the poison of ____. (Job 20:16)
21. All the Chaldeans, Pekod, and ____, and Koa. (Ezek. 23:23)
22. In the midst of the church will I ____ praise. (Heb. 2:12)
23. Therefore thou ____ inexcusable, O man. (Rom. 2:1)
25. Lobster box.
26. Do not ____ his dwelling place. (Prov. 24:15 NIV)
27. Vapor (comb. form).
28. Stood a Lamb as it had ____ slain. (Rev. 5:6)
30. To deceive the nations . . . in the four quarters of the earth, ____ and Magog. (Rev. 20:8)
31. ____ is he that cometh in the name of the Lord. (Mark 11:9)
33. Common contraction.

34. Mordecai the Jew, who ___ at the king's gate. (Esther 6:10 NIV)
35. Daniel was taken up out of the ____. (Dan. 6:23)
36. I see men as ____, walking. (Mark 8:24)
37. The children of ____ of Hezekiah, ninety and eight. (Ezra 2:16)
38. ____ hairs are here and there upon him, yet he knoweth not. (Hos. 7:9)
39. Certain ____ every day, . . . according to the commandment of Moses. (2 Chron. 8:13)
40. When he had taken him in his ____. (Mark 9:36)
42. Federal accounting division.
43. And the sons of Bela . . . Uzziel, and Jerimoth, and ____. (1 Chron. 7:7)
44. The Spirit, and the water, and the blood: and these three agree in ____. (1 John 5:8)
45. Andrew his brother, casting a ____ into the sea. (Matt. 4:18)

27

Across

1. He . . . lifts the needy from the ____ heap. (1 Sam. 2:8 NIV)
4. The name of the ____ is called Wormwood. (Rev. 8:11)
8. He who loveth God love his brother ____. (1 John 4:21)
12. The sons of Caleb . . . : ____, Elah, and Naam. (1 Chron. 4:15)
13. A ____ of every unclean and hateful bird. (Rev. 18:2)
14. One of the people might lightly have ____ with thy wife. (Gen. 26:10)
15. Russian Scandinavians.
16. When your ____ is fulfilled. (2 Cor. 10:6)
18. There be upon the ____ of the horses, HOLINESS. (Zech. 14:20)
20. Waste allowances.
21. Rio ____, U.S. border river.
23. The course of nature; and it is ____ on fire of hell. (James 3:6)
24. Milk and honey, which is the glory of all ____. (Ezek. 20:6)
25. Jacob sojourned in the land of ____. (Ps. 105:23)
26. O thou man of God, there is death in the ____. (2 Kings 4:40)
29. You should not use outward ____ to make yourselves beautiful. (1 Peter 3:3 GNB)
30. He brake the withs, as a thread of ____ is broken. (Judg. 16:9)
31. ____ obeyed Abraham, calling him lord. (1 Peter 3:6)
32. Dentist's degree.
33. The ____ of truth shall be established for ever. (Prov. 12:19)
34. ____ answered him, Lord, to whom shall we go? (John 6:68)
35. Riblah, on the east side of ____. (Num. 34:11)
36. In the midst of the church will I sing ____. (Heb. 2:12)
37. A day of the trumpet and ____. (Zeph. 1:16)
40. And the day star ____ in your hearts. (2 Peter 1:19)
41. The waters ____ continually until the tenth month. (Gen. 8:5)
43. As it was in the days of ____, so shall it be. (Luke 17:26)
46. He set it up in the plain of ____. (Dan. 3:1)
47. ____ it, even to the foundation thereof. (Ps. 137:7)
48. It is certain we ____ carry nothing out. (1 Tim. 6:7)
49. South African yoke.
50. Thy King cometh, sitting on an ____' colt. (John 12:15)
51. How long will it be ____ they attain to innocency? (Hos. 8:5)

Down

1. So fight I, not as one that beateth the ____. (1 Cor. 9:26)
2. Theatre notice.
3. ____, love your wives, even as Christ also loved the church. (Eph. 5:25)
4. Censures.
5. Let their ____ be made a snare, and a trap. (Rom. 11:9)
6. The mystery which hath been hid from ____ and from generations. (Col. 1:26)
7. Wherefore art thou ____ in thine apparel? (Isa. 63:2)
8. Be self-controlled and ____. (1 Peter 5:8 NIV)
9. Judgment also will I lay to the ____. (Isa. 28:17)
10. After the most straitest ____ of our religion. (Acts 26:5)
11. Give to drink unto one of these little ____ a cup of cold water. (Matt. 10:42)
17. Unclean, whether it is any ____ of wood or clothing or skin or sack. (Lev. 11:32 NKJV)
19. Thou shouldest be for salvation unto the ____ of the earth. (Acts 13:47)
21. We are ____, when we are weak. (2 Cor. 13:9)
22. David's men and Joab returned from a ____. (2 Sam. 3:22 NIV)
23. I ____ three unclean spirits like frogs. (Rev. 16:13)
25. Insects are unclean, except those that ____. (Lev. 11:20 GNB)
26. But let ____ have her perfect work. (James 1:4)
27. Mined materials.
28. Straightway the spirit ____ him. (Mark 9:20)

30. Purge away thy dross, take away all thy ____. (Isa. 1:25)
31. The gathering together of the waters called he ____. (Gen. 1:10)
33. He burned the bones of the king of Edom into ____. (Amos 2:1)
34. Vanities.
35. ____ thyself with glory and beauty. (Job 40:10)
36. I ____ toward the mark for the prize. (Phil. 3:14)

37. The fear of the Lord ____ length to life. (Prov. 10:27 NIV)
38. White or colorless (comb. form).
39. An half ____ of land, which a yoke of oxen might plow. (1 Sam. 14:14)
40. Nevertheless ____ heart was perfect. (1 Kings 15:14)
42. Pepper plant, Borneo.
44. Paddle.
45. Direction: Caesarea to Agrippina.

28

Across

1. He ____ on the ground, and made clay of the spittle. (John 9:6)
5. They hatch cockatrice' eggs, and weave the spider's ____. (Isa. 59:5)
8. You sold your people for a pittance, gaining nothing from their ____. (Ps. 44:12 NIV)
12. You will be protected from the ____ of the tongue. (Job 5:21 NIV)
13. Stand in ____, and sin not. (Ps. 4:4)
14. Ireland.
15. Shammah the son of ____ the Hararite. (2 Sam. 23:11)
16. Every high priest is ____ from among men. (Heb. 5:1 NIV)
18. A little ____ works through the whole batch. (Gal. 5:9 NIV)
20. Alone.
21. I will be his God, and he shall be my ____. (Rev. 21:7)
23. Pray ye that your flight be not in the ____. (Matt. 24:20)
27. Their tongue ____ through the earth. (Ps. 73:9 NASB)
31. Short proverb.
32. Yellow dye plant.
33. ____ is a liar but he that denieth that Jesus is the Christ? (1 John 2:22)
35. Scottish weight machine.
36. Pacific Island group.
38. With least resistance.
40. Instead of fragrance there will be a ____. (Isa. 3:24 NIV)
42. Molasses liquor.
43. Frosts.
45. The house he builds is like a ____ cocoon. (Job 27:18 NIV)
49. The whole ____ groaneth and travaileth in pain together until now. (Rom. 8:22)
53. The knowledge of him ____ hath called us to glory and virtue. (2 Peter 1:3)
54. You ____ wages, only to put them in a purse with holes. (Hag. 1:6 NIV)
55. As the chased ____, and as a sheep that no man taketh up. (Isa. 13:14)
56. Sister and wife of Zeus.
57. Fennel.
58. Airport code for Stuttgart, Germany.
59. His parents went to Jerusalem every ____. (Luke 2:41)

Down

1. Arise, Peter; ____ and eat. (Acts 11:7)
2. Literary leaf.
3. I saw as it were ____ ____ of glass mingled with fire. (Rev. 15:2)
4. And of the ____, Aristarchus and Secundus. (Acts 20:4)
5. A servant, and ____ made in the likeness of men. (Phil. 2:7)
6. From following the ____ great with young. (Ps. 78:71)
7. You are from ____, I am from above. (John 8:23 NASB)
8. Four-chapter New Testament book.
9. As thou, Father, ____ in me, and I in thee. (John 17:21)
10. And whosoever loveth and maketh a ____. (Rev. 22:15)
11. To this ____ I was born, and for this cause. (John 18:37)
17. Lamb's pen name.
19. Thick foliage.
22. To make in himself of twain one ____ man. (Eph. 2:15)
24. Straightway the spirit ____ him; and he fell. (Mark 9:20)
25. Inner selves.
26. To fill it up taketh from the garment, and the ____ is made worse. (Matt. 9:16)
27. As the flower of the grass he shall ____ away. (James 1:10)
28. Some men came carrying a paralytic on ____ ____. (Luke 5:18 NIV)
29. Hoarfrost.
30. If the husband be dead, ____ is loosed from the law. (Rom. 7:2)
34. Blade.
37. Bookkeeper's abbreviation.
39. The sepulchre that Abraham bought for a ____. (Acts 7:16)
41. As being ____ together of the grace of life. (1 Peter 3:7)

44. Take handfuls of ____ from a furnace. (Exod. 9:8 NIV)
46. The bowels of the saints are refreshed by ____. (Philem. 7)
47. Brought them unto Halah, and Habor, and ____. (1 Chron. 5:26)
48. For one ____ differeth from another. (1 Cor. 15:41)
49. Economic council's initials.
50. Then arose Peter, and ____ unto the sepulchre. (Luke 24:12)
51. Of ____, the family of the Erites. (Num. 26:16)
52. Abner, the son of ____, Saul's uncle. (1 Sam. 14:50)

29

Across

1. Woe unto thee, ____! thou art undone. (Num. 21:29)
5. ____ had an army of men that bare targets and spears. (2 Chron. 14:8)
8. Behold, my belly is as wine which hath no ____. (Job 32:19)
12. The holy scriptures, which are ____ to make thee wise unto salvation. (2 Tim. 3:15)
13. His eyes shall be ____ with wine. (Gen. 49:12)
14. Sibbecai the Hushathite, ____ the Ahohite. (1 Chron. 11:29)
15. Felt indignantly aggrieved.
17. Dotted, as with stars or flowers.
18. "Come, let us ____ him."
19. When the commandment came, sin ____, and I died. (Rom. 7:9)
21. ____ the son of Ikkesh the Tekoite. (1 Chron. 11:28)
23. The people shall go out and gather a certain ____ every day. (Exod 16:4)
24. Ye have heard of the patience of ____. (James 5:11)
27. "How much do you ____ my master?" (Luke 16:5 NIV)
29. The patriarch Abraham gave the ____ of the spoils. (Heb. 7:4)
32. "What ____ you, Hagar? Fear not." (Gen. 21:17 NKJV)
34. There is a ____ here, which hath five barley loaves. (John 6:9)
36. We ____ not make ourselves of the number. (2 Cor. 10:12)
37. He destroyed their vines with hail and their sycamore-figs with ____. (Ps. 78:47 NIV)
39. Unclean for you the weasel, the ____. (Lev. 11:29 NIV)
41. With (prefix).
42. No man shall ____ me of this boasting. (2 Cor. 11:10)
44. Their bows will ____ down the young men. (Isa. 13:18 NASB)
46. Hath appointed me another seed ____ of Abel. (Gen. 4:25)
49. South Pacific island group.
53. They ____ not, neither do they spin. (Matt. 6:28)

Down

54. Give meat for ____ to the priest. (1 Sam. 2:15 NKJV)
56. Second wife of Henry VIII.
57. Pochereth of Zebaim, the children of ____. (Ezra 2:57)
58. Noun suffix.
59. He was dead already, they brake not his ____. (John 19:33)
60. Not willing to make ____ a publick example. (Matt. 1:19)
61. He measured the city with the ____. (Rev. 21:16)

Down

1. Call me not Naomi, call me ____. (Ruth 1:20)
2. The son of Jesse, which was the son of ____. (Luke 3:32)
3. I ____ will keep thee from the hour of temptation. (Rev. 3:10)
4. Hosea, the son of ____. (Hos.1:1)
5. If thou let this man go, thou ____ not Caesar's friend. (John 19:12)
6. A Prophet was beforetime called a ____. (1 Sam. 9:9)
7. They are like the deaf ____ that stoppeth her ear. (Ps. 58:4)
8. That God hath ____ his people. (Luke 7:16)
9. He appeared unto the ____ ____ they sat at meat. (Mark 16:14)
10. Anointing him with oil in the ____ of the Lord. (James 5:14)
11. Ye shall find a colt ____, whereon never man sat. (Mark 11:2)
16. When Paul was brought before ____. (2 Tim. Subscript)
20. When anyone went to a wine ____ to draw fifty measures. (Hag. 2:16 NIV)
22. Take an ____ and push it through his ear lobe. (Deut. 15:17 NIV)
24. Disciple's name (abbrev.).
25. Give us of your ____; for our lamps are gone out. (Matt. 25:8)
26. The fulness of the ____ of the gospel of Christ. (Rom. 15:29)
28. He touched his ____, and healed him. (Luke 22:51)
30. The fire shall ____ every man's work. (1 Cor. 3:13)

31. To ____ the son of Zephaniah. (Zech. 6:14)
33. He ____ the barren woman in her home. (Ps. 113:9 NIV)
35. Thou shalt in any wise let the ____ go. (Deut. 22:7)
38. Upon the great ____ of their right foot. (Exod. 29:20)
40. Though the waves thereof ____ themselves. (Jer. 5:22)
43. Avim, and ____, and Ophrah. (Josh. 18:23)
45. Except a man be born of ____ and of the Spirit. (John 3:5)
46. Rome's country (abbrev.).
47. Fear ____ of those things which thou shalt suffer. (Rev. 2:10)
48. God made a ____, and it separated the water. (Gen. 1:6 GNB)
50. I believe; help thou ____ unbelief. (Mark 9:24)
51. Christ also hath ____ suffered for sins. (1 Peter 3:18)
52. Being such an one as Paul the ____. (Philem. 9)
55. The sun and the ____ were darkened by reason of the smoke. (Rev. 9:2)

30

Across

1. Water vehicle.
5. _____; and he smelleth the battle afar. (Job 39:25)
9. Shamed, who built Ono, and ____. (1 Chron. 8:12)
12. Lamech said unto his wives, ____ and Zillah. (Gen. 4:23)
13. Greek coin.
14. The same love, being of ____ accord. (Phil. 2:2)
15. The ____ that is in thy brother's eye. (Luke 6:42)
16. An he goat came from the ____. (Dan. 8:5)
17. Out of whose womb came the ____? (Job 38:29)
18. Hasten.
20. For I have ____, in whatsoever state I am. (Phil. 4:11)
22. I labor, struggling with all his ____. (Col. 1:29 NIV)
25. Brazilian parrot.
26. Persian gateway.
27. Lest Satan should ____ an advantage of us. (2 Cor. 2:11)
29. A wise king ____ out the wicked. (Prov. 20:26 NKJV)
33. The swan, and the pelican, and the ____ eagle. (Lev. 11:18)
35. In all things ye are ____ superstitious. (Acts 17:22)
37. Eucalyptus sap.
38. Submit yourselves unto the ____. (1 Peter 5:5)
40. Waiting for the adoption, to ____, the redemption of our body. (Romans 8:23)
42. Uzzi and Uzziel, and Jerimoth, and ____. (1 Chron. 7:7)
43. Architects organization.
45. ____, O isles, unto me; and hearken, ye people. (Isa. 49:1)
47. Earnestly I seek you; my soul ____ for you. (Ps. 63:1 NIV)
51. Ordinal numbers (comb. form).
52. To meet the Lord in the ____: and so shall we ever be with the Lord. (1 Thess. 4:17)
53. He went down and dwelt in the top of the rock ____. (Judg. 15:8)

55. Is blind, and cannot see ____ off. (2 Peter 1:9)
58. ____ the son of Ikkesh the Tekoite. (1 Chron. 27:9)
59. We spend our years as a ____ that is told. (Ps. 90:9)
60. He shall have put down all ____ and all authority. (1 Cor. 15:24)
61. If ye be ____ of the Spirit, ye are not under the law. (Gal. 5:18)
62. Did ____ the Beth-elite build Jericho. (1 Kings 16:34)
63. Flowed smoothly.

Down

1. Abraham went and took the ____, and offered him up. (Gen. 22:13)
2. Why make ye this ____, and weep? (Mark 5:39)
3. You deserted the Rock, who ____ you? (Deut. 32:18 NIV)
4. Barnabas also was carried away with ____ dissimulation. (Gal. 2:13)
5. ____ great a matter a little fire kindleth! (James 3:5)
6. By faith ____ offered unto God a more excellent sacrifice. (Heb. 11:4)
7. The Lord said to ____, Go, take unto thee a wife. (Hos. 1:2)
8. Killed thy prophets, and digged down thine ____. (Rom. 11:3)
9. And made themselves ____ coverings. (Gen. 3:7 NASB)
10. Christ also hath ____ suffered for sins. (1 Peter 3:18)
11. Let us not love in word, neither in tongue; but in ____ and in truth. (1 John 3:18)
19. If he shall ask an ____, will he offer him a scorpion? (Luke 11:12)
21. He wrote also letters to ____ on the Lord. (2 Chron. 32:17)
22. They shall fall by the ____ of the sword. (Luke 21:24)
23. Heber's wife took a ____ of the tent. (Judg. 4:21)
24. They should rest ____ for a little season. (Rev. 6:11)
28. He brake the withs, as a thread of ____ is broken when it toucheth the fire. (Judg. 16:9)

30. The Lord thy God, he is God, the ____ God. (Deut. 7:9)
31. The devil threw him down, and ____ him. (Luke 9:42)
32. They toil not, neither do they ____. (Matt. 6:28)
34. Wilt thou ____ it up in three days? (John 2:20)
36. My head with ____ thou didst not anoint. (Luke 7:46)
39. He ____ from supper, and laid aside his garments. (John 13:4)
41. ____ the kine to the cart. (1 Sam. 6:7)
44. Gave his daughter to Jarha his servant to wife; and she bare him ____. (1 Chron. 2:35)

46. Wandering ____, to whom is reserved the blackness. (Jude 13)
47. And his ____ drew the third part of the stars. (Rev. 12:4)
48. The labourer is worthy of his ____. (Luke 10:7)
49. Unto Enoch was born ____. (Gen. 4:18)
50. That which cometh of the ____ of his patrimony. (Deut. 18:8)
54. Honey.
56. Arab name.
57. Wherefore art thou ____ in thine apparel. (Isa. 63:2)

31

Across

1. Shall I ____ from Abraham that thing which I do? (Gen. 18:17)
5. I wish I could be with you now and change my ____. (Gal. 4:20 NIV)
9. God ____ every thing that he had made, and, behold it was very good. (Gen. 1:31)
12. Tubal-cain, an instructer of every artificer in brass and ____. (Gen. 4:22)
13. The ruler of that ____ . . . took her. (Gen. 34:2 NIV)
14. Commotion.
15. Into the wilderness four thousand men that were ____. (Acts 21:38)
17. I cannot redeem it, lest I ____ mine own inheritance. (Ruth 4:6)
18. Though ye have ____ among the pots. (Ps. 68:13)
19. Delivered first this psalm to ____ the Lord. (1 Chron. 16:7)
21. Whoever ____ this edict, let a timber be pulled from his house. (Ezra 6:11 NKJV)
24. Neither count I my life ____ unto myself. (Acts 20:24)
25. Naphtali is a hind let ____. (Gen. 49:21)
26. O ____, we came indeed down at the first time. (Gen. 43:20)
27. Girl's name.
30. The poison of ____ is under their lips. (Rom. 3:13)
31. ____ shall be a serpent by the way. (Gen. 49:17)
32. Roman road.
33. Better . . . that a millstone were hanged about his neck, and he cast into the ____. (Luke 17:2)
34. Can a ____ tree, my brethren, bear olive berries? (James 3:12)
35. Every one of you hath a ____, hath a doctrine. (1 Cor. 14:26)
36. Death rattle.
38. Bernard's alias.
39. Like men condemned to die in the ____. (1 Cor. 4:9 NIV)
41. Operatic solo.
42. Joshua the son of ____, the servant of the Lord. (Judg. 2:8)
43. ____ saith unto him, How can a man be born when he is old? (John 3:4)
48. At thy word I will let down the ____. (Luke 5:5)
49. Malay dagger.
50. There should be mockers in the ____ time. (Jude 18)
51. Issachar is a strong ____ crouching down. (Gen. 49:14)
52. We are troubled on every ____, yet not distressed. (2 Cor. 4:8)
53. Their ____ of pleasure is to carouse in broad daylight. (2 Peter 2:13 NIV)

Down

1. Predestinated according to the purpose of ____. (Eph. 1:11)
2. The sons of Caleb the son of Jephunneh; ____. (1 Chron. 4:15)
3. The son of Abinadab, in all the region of ____. (1 Kings 4:11)
4. Neither give heed to fables and ____ genealogies. (1 Tim. 1:4)
5. Gather ye together first the ____. (Matt. 13:30)
6. Ram the firstborn, and Bunah, and ____. (1 Chron. 2:25)
7. ____ begat Kish, and Kish begat Saul. (1 Chron. 8:33)
8. Intending after ____ to bring him forth. (Acts 12:4)
9. A certain ____, as he journeyed, came where he was. (Luke 10:33)
10. Moslem call to prayer.
11. If any would not ____, neither should he eat. (2 Thess. 3:10)
16. Ireland (Gaelic).
20. ____, and he smelleth the battle afar off. (Job 39:25)
21. ____ for the day! for the day of the Lord. (Joel 1:15)
22. I say unto you, he shall in no wise ____ his reward. (Matt. 10:42)
23. Blasphemers, disobedient ____ ____, unthankful, unholy. (2 Tim. 3:2)
24. Jerusalem's splendor, her multitude, her ____ of revelry. (Isa. 5:14 NASB)
26. If a man is lazy, the rafters ____. (Eccles. 10:18 NIV)

28. Cancel.
29. To make war against him that sat on the horse, and against his ____. (Rev. 19:19)
31. To live is Christ, and to ____ is gain. (Phil. 1:21)
32. Resident of Israel.
34. And maketh collops of fat on his ____. (Job 15:27)
35. Till thou hast ____ the uttermost farthing. (Matt. 5:26)
37. Set forth as ____ example, suffering the vengeance. (Jude 7)

38. Porridge (Scottish).
39. There was one ____, a prophetess. (Luke 2:36)
40. Feels remorse.
41. Tart.
44. Fifth son of Bela. (1 Chron. 7:7)
45. Much learning doth make thee ____. (Acts 26:24)
46. ____ a little wine for thy stomach's sake. (1 Tim. 5:23)
47. Musical direction.

32

Across

1. Squirrel skin.
5. They said unto her, Thou art ____. (Acts 12:15)
8. Ye shall in no ____ enter into the kingdom. (Matt 5:20)
12. Of ____, the son of Bani, the son of Shamer. (1 Chron. 6:46)
13. We ____ great plainness of speech. (2 Cor. 3:12)
14. Doth God take care for ____? (1 Cor. 9:9)
15. Puppeteer.
16. The ____ sitting upon the young, or upon the eggs. (Deut. 22:6)
17. My God shall supply all your ____. (Phil. 4:19)
18. ____ had waited till Job had spoken. (Job 32:4)
20. Believed they his words; they ____ his praise. (Ps. 106:12)
22. Three (comb. form).
24. If anyone ____, he should do it with the strength God provides. (1 Peter 4:11 NIV)
28. Prophesy not unto us right things, speak unto us smooth things, prophesy ____. (Isa. 30:10)
32. They that ____ networks, shall be confounded. (Isa. 19:9)
33. Irish exclamation.
34. The trees of the Lord are full of ____. (Ps. 104:16)
36. The swan, and the pelican, and the ____ eagle. (Lev. 11:18)
37. Secundus; and ____ of Derbe, and Timotheus. (Acts 20:4)
39. French painter (1839–1906).
41. Knowledge attained through faith alone.
43. I went down to the orchard of ____ trees to see the blossoms. (Song of Sol. 6:11 NASB)
44. With Zebedee their father, mending their ____. (Matt. 4:21)
46. See, the Lord ____ on a swift cloud. (Isa. 19:1 NIV)
50. The price of his ____ shall be according unto the number of years. (Lev. 25:50)
53. To him that overcometh will I give to ____ of the hidden manna. (Rev. 2:17)
55. Shield border.
56. If he has done you any wrong or ____ you anything, charge it to me. (Philem. 18 NIV)

57. By grace ye ____ saved. (Eph. 2:5)
58. These are a smoke in my ____. (Isa. 65:5)
59. Dampens.
60. God hath judged me . . . therefore called she his name ____. (Gen. 30:6)
61. Have they not ____? have they not divided the prey? (Judg. 5:30)

Down

1. It is worth more than gold, than a gold ____. (Job 28:17 GNB)
2. Zophah, and Imna, and Shelesh, and ____. (1 Chron. 7:35)
3. The fourth to ____, he, his sons, and his brethren, were twelve. (1 Chron. 25:11)
4. A new earth, wherein dwelleth ____. (2 Peter 3:13)
5. Jeremiah sank down into the ____. (Jer. 38:6 NIV)
6. Nevertheless, ____'_ heart was perfect. (1 Kings 15:14)
7. ____ hath forsaken me, having loved this present world. (2 Tim. 4:10)
8. In the ____ will I bless the Lord. (Ps. 26:12)
9. Now also the ____ is laid unto the root. (Luke 3:9)
10. They shall ____ his face; and his name shall be in their foreheads. (Rev. 22:4)
11. Whose ____ is destruction, whose God is their belly. (Phil. 3:19)
19. Bezaleel the son of ____. (Exod. 31:2)
21. Behold, I make all things ____. (Rev. 21:5)
23. That which groweth of ____ own accord. (Lev. 25:5)
25. O ____ man, that faith without works is dead. (James 2:20)
26. The Lord rebuke thee, O Satan; ____ the Lord. (Zech. 3:2)
27. Withered.
28. Pistol.
29. Of ____, the family of the Eranites. (Num. 26:36)
30. Ram-headed (comb. form).
31. Pouch.
35. The sin of Judah is written with a ____ of iron. (Jer. 17:1)
38. You (German).

40. Cozbi, the daughter of ____. (Num. 25:15)
42. That in thy ____ he might have ministered unto me. (Philem. 13)
45. ____ obeyed Abraham, calling him lord. (1 Peter 3:6)
47. My doctrine shall ____ as the rain. (Deut. 32:2)
48. Repent; or ____ I will come unto thee quickly. (Rev. 2:16)

49. Being born again, not of corruptible ____. (1 Peter 1:23)
50. Sir, didst thou not ____ good seed? (Matt. 13:27)
51. Stand in ____, and sin not. (Ps. 4:4)
52. ____ us love one another for love is of God. (1 John 4:7)
54. Were there not ____ cleansed? but where are the nine? (Luke 17:17)

33

Across

1. There is _____ here, which hath five barley loaves. (John 6:9)
5. Go to the Philistines to get their plows, ____, . . . sharpened. (1 Sam. 13:20 GNB)
9. Nigerian tribe.
12. As he passed by, he saw ____ the son of Alphaeus. (Mark 2:14)
13. Naum, which was the son of ____. (Luke 3:25)
14. He regarded the ____ estate of his handmaiden. (Luke 1:48)
15. Lo, in her mouth was an olive ____. (Gen. 8:11)
16. Does not keep a tight ____ on his tongue. (James 1:26 NIV)
17. Pierce his ear with an ____. (Exod. 21:6 NIV)
18. But now being made ____ from sin. (Rom. 6:22)
20. And put my finger into the print of the ____. (John 20:25)
22. I believe everything that ____ with the Law. (Acts 24:14 NIV)
25. When the ____ heard it, they were moved with indignation. (Matt. 20:24)
26. I ____ thy voice in the garden. (Gen. 3:10)
27. The sun and the ____ were darkened. (Rev. 9:2)
28. My heart standeth in ____ of thy word. (Ps. 119:161)
31. I will strengthen the ____ of the king. (Ezek. 30:24)
32. Every ____ that useth milk is unskilful in the word. (Heb. 5:13)
33. Albanian river.
34. Low (French).
35. Having the key of the bottomless ____. (Rev. 20:1)
36. Tendency.
37. Love worketh no ____ to his neighbour. (Rom 13:10)
38. He ____ the winepress of the fury of the wrath of God. (Rev. 19:15 NIV)
39. The Father, the Word, and the Holy Ghost: and ____ three are one. (1 John 5:7)
42. In three ____ I will raise it up. (John 2:19)
43. ____ me, and deliver me from the hand of strange children. (Ps. 144:11)
44. ____ was not deceived, but the woman. (1 Tim. 2:14)
46. They were stoned, they were ____ asunder. (Heb. 11:37)
50. Copper is smelted from ____. (Job 28:2 NIV)
51. A ____ vision has been shown to me. (Isa. 21:2 NIV)
52. Jacob I loved, but ____ I hated. (Rom. 9:13 NIV)
53. But ye have made it a ____ of thieves. (Matt 11:17)
54. Jesus Christ of the ____ of David. (2 Tim. 2:8)
55. Till a ____ strike through his liver. (Prov. 7:23)

Down

1. And so ____ Israel shall be saved. (Rom. 11:26)
2. We sailed to the ____ of Crete. (Acts 27:7 NIV)
3. The king of Assyria brought men from Babylon, . . . Cuthah, and . . . ____. (2 Kings 17:24)
4. And star ____ from star in splendor. (1 Cor. 15:41 NIV)
5. The Amorites would dwell in mount ____ in Aijalon. (Judg. 1:35)
6. As he saith also in ____, I will call them my people, which were not my people. (Rom. 9:25)
7. ____ perceived that the Lord had called the child. (1 Sam. 3:8)
8. Likewise joy shall be in heaven over one ____ that repenteth. (Luke 15:7)
9. Sibbecai the Hushathite, ____, the Ahohite. (1 Chron. 11:29)
10. The silver cord be loosed, or the golden ____ be broken. (Eccles. 12:6)
11. I am a brother to dragons, and a companion to ____. (Job 30:29)
19. Bring thee a ____ heifer without spot. (Num. 19:2)
21. But a son; and if a son, then ____ heir of God. (Gal. 4:7)
22. ____ told Jezebel all that Elijah had done. (1 Kings 19:1)
23. Shimei the son of ____ fell down before the king. (2 Sam. 19:18)
24. Let seven priests bear seven trumpets of ____ horns. (Josh. 6:6)

25. ____ the kine to the cart, and bring their calves. (1 Sam. 6:7)
27. Picnic pest.
28. He made a whip out of cords, and drove all from the temple ____. (John 2:15 NIV)
29. The ____ bloweth where it listeth. (John 3:8)
30. The ____ of the earth were afraid, drew near. (Isa. 41:5)
32. Give us of your ____; for our lamps are gone out. (Matt. 25:8)
33. Bringeth forth herbs meet for them by whom it is ____. (Heb. 6:7)
35. No one calls for justice; no one ____ his case. (Isa. 59:4 NIV)
36. To ____ them that dwell upon the earth. (Rev. 3:10)
37. No prophecy of the scripture ____ of any private interpretation. (2 Peter 1:20)

38. And hath been ____ of mankind. (James 3:7)
39. Will you keep to the old path that evil men have ____? (Job 22:15 NIV)
40. The labourer is worthy of his ____. (Luke 10:7)
41. Him that holdeth the sceptre from the house of ____. (Amos 1:5)
42. We ____ not make ourselves of the number. (2 Cor. 10:12)
45. It is appointed unto men once to ____. (Heb. 9:27)
47. Ben-hadad hearkened unto king ____. (2 Chron. 16:4)
48. Fleshly lusts, which ____ against the soul. (1 Peter 2:11)
49. I went down to the grove of ____ trees. (Song of Sol. 6:11 NIV)

34

Across

1. The dust hardens into a ____. (Job 38:38 NASB)
5. For the glory of God ____ lighten it. (Rev. 21:23)
8. Therein is the righteousness of God revealed ____ faith to faith. (Rom. 1:17)
12. After him was Shammah the son of ____. (2 Sam. 23:11)
13. Every ____ shall see him. (Rev. 1:7)
14. I will ____ Sisera, the commander of Jabin's army. (Judg. 4:7 NIV)
15. See where thou hast not been ____ with. (Jer. 3:2)
16. ____, which was the son of Noe. (Luke 3:36)
17. Fine ____ have been poured upon me. (Ps. 92:10 NIV)
18. To infuriate.
20. Makes amends.
22. The Valley of Siddim was full of ____ pits. (Gen. 14:10 NIV)
23. Dwelt in the land of ____, on the east of Eden. (Gen. 4:16)
24. Thou shalt utterly ____ it (an abomination). (Deut. 7:26)
27. ____ the sincere milk of the word. (1 Peter 2:2)
31. ____ no man any thing but to love one another. (Rom. 13:8)
32. Scrap of cloth.
33. I will ____ them from death. (Hos. 13:14)
37. ____ ye have purified your souls in obeying the truth. (1 Peter 1:22)
40. Direction: Jerusalem to Caesarea.
41. ____ unrighteousness is sin. (1 John 5:17)
42. No one calls for justice; no one ____ his case with integrity. (Isa. 59:4 NIV)
45. He ____ the man of God had said. (2 Kings 7:17)
49. The precious blood of Christ, as of a ____. (1 Peter 1:19)
50. Be not, as the hypocrites, of a ____ countenance. (Matt. 6:16)
52. I am the true ____, and my Father is the husbandman. (John 15:1)
53. Eleasah his son, ____ his son. (1 Chron. 8:37)
54. Sir, come down ____ my child die. (John 4:49)
55. Sicilian resort.

56. Take my ____ upon you, and learn of me. (Matt. 11:29)
57. To be (Spanish).
58. Let us draw ____ with a true heart. (Heb. 10:22)

Down

1. Every ____ that openeth the womb shall be called holy to the Lord. (Luke 2:23)
2. For ____ and for a snare to the inhabitants of Jerusalem. (Isa. 8:14)
3. Samuel answered Saul, and said, I am the ____. (1 Sam. 9:19)
4. All the ____ of the children of Israel. (Acts 5:21)
5. This is a ____ place, and the time is now past. (Matt. 14:15)
6. They . . . camped at ____-abarim, at the border of Moab. (Num. 33:44 NASB)
7. The ____ by the word of the holy ones. (Dan. 4:17)
8. The ____ came, and the winds blew, and beat upon that house. (Matt. 7:27)
9. And the ____ of that house was great. (Luke 6:49)
10. Shield border.
11. Benjamin's ____ was five times so much as any of their's. (Gen. 43:34)
19. Third state of matter.
21. Upon the great ____ of their right foot. (Exod. 29:20)
24. Nor the inhabitants of ____ and her towns. (Judg. 1:27)
25. The poor man had nothing, save one little ____ lamb. (2 Sam. 12:3)
26. Spread to dry.
28. Fifth son of Bela. (1 Chron 7:7)
29. ____, and fell on his neck, and kissed him. (Luke 15:20)
30. Is there any taste in the white of an ____? (Job 6:6)
34. And to ____ us to serve him without fear. (Luke 1:74 NIV)
35. The ____ of your faith, even the salvation. (1 Peter 1:9)
36. He took and sent ____ unto them from before him. (Gen. 43:34)
37. More unhappy.

38. The two sons of ____, Hophni and Phinehas. (1 Sam. 1:3)
39. He was numbered with the ____ apostles. (Acts 1:26)
42. The people sat down to eat and drink, and rose up to ____. (1 Cor. 10:7)
43. Lariat.
44. The valley of Jiphthah-el toward the north side of Beth- ____. (Josh. 19:27)

46. Jesus saith unto them, Come and ____. (John 21:12)
47. ____ a prophetess, the daughter of Phanuel. (Luke 2:36)
48. Scorch.
51. Ye also, as lively stones, ____ built up a spiritual house. (1 Peter 2:5)

35

Across

1. Heber, which was the son of ____. (Luke 3:35)
5. ____ yourselves likewise with the same mind. (1 Peter 4:1)
8. Men of Judah went to the top of the rock ____. (Judg. 15:11)
12. Nevertheless ____ heart was perfect. (1 Kings 15:14)
13. Extinct bird.
14. Ye ____ men with burdens grievous to be borne. (Luke 11:46)
15. Flowery garlands.
16. David sent messengers to ____ -bosheth Saul's son. (2 Sam. 3:14)
17. They came unto the ____ gate that leadeth unto the city. (Acts 12:10)
18. The ____ are the children of the wicked one. (Matt. 13:38)
20. ____ that great city Babylon, that mighty city! (Rev. 18:10)
22. The wicked desireth the ____ of evil men. (Prov. 12:12)
24. Michael, and Obadiah, and Joel, ____, five. (1 Chron. 7:3)
28. Are ye unworthy to judge the smallest ____? (1 Cor. 6:2)
32. A certain maid beheld him as he ____ ____ the fire. (Luke 22:56)
33. He planteth an ____, and the rain doth nourish it. (Isa. 44:14)
34. ____, verily, their sound went into all the earth. (Rom. 10:18)
36. Shade tree.
37. Draw thee waters for the ____. (Nah. 3:14)
40. There came ____ ____ from the east. (Matt. 2:1)
43. And thou shalt have no more sooth-____. (Mic. 5:12)
45. Natural red dye.
46. Because he did the things that were commanded him? I ____ not. (Luke 17:9)
48. Bashan and Carmel wither, and the flower of Lebanon ____. (Nah. 1:4 NKJV)
52. God remembered ____ and every living thing. (Gen. 8:1)
55. We do not ____ after the flesh. (2 Cor. 10:3)
57. Shimri, and ____ his brother, the Tizite. (1 Chron. 11:45)
58. The Pharisees began to ____ him vehemently. (Luke 11:53)
59. Of ____, the family of the Erites. (Num. 26:16)
60. Sick of a fever, and ____ they tell him of her. (Mark 1:30)
61. Never (Poetic).
62. The first came out ____, all over like a hairy garment. (Gen. 25:25)
63. Suffer us to go away into the ____ of swine. (Matt. 8:31)

Down

1. Let your speech be alway with grace, seasoned with ____. (Col. 4:6)
2. I saw as it were ____ ____ of glass. (Rev. 15:2)
3. A lion has come out of his ____. (Jer. 4:7 NIV)
4. Behold, the prophets declare good to the king with one ____. (2 Chron. 18:12)
5. Pochereth of Zebaim, the children of ____. (Ezra 2:57)
6. Rose genus.
7. Of ____ came Eleazar, who had no sons. (1 Chron. 24:28)
8. Elijah said unto ____, Tarry here. (2 Kings 2:2)
9. She got a papyrus basket for him and coated it with ____ and pitch. (Exod. 2:3 NIV)
10. Tumult.
11. Holy ____ of God spake as they were moved by the Holy Ghost. (2 Peter 1:21)
19. Your young men shall ____ visions. (Acts 2:17)
21. Thy King cometh unto thee, meek, and sitting upon an ____. (Matt. 21:5)
23. The fiery trial which is to ____ you. (1 Peter 4:12)
25. Whatever ____ it is, in which any work is done. (Lev. 11:32 NKJV)
26. The engrafted word, which is ____ to save your souls. (James 1:21)
27. When they had sung an ____, they went out. (Mark 14:26)
28. Many slain, a ____ of corpses. (Nah. 3:3 NASB)
29. The churches of ____ salute you. (1 Cor. 16:19)

30. So that ____ are without excuse. (Rom. 1:20)
31. Woe to the women that ____ pillows to all armholes. (Ezek. 13:18)
35. The children of Keros, the children of ____. (Neh. 7:47)
38. Uz, and Hul, and ____, and Mash. (Gen. 10:23)
39. Ye do ____, not knowing the scriptures. (Matt. 22:29)
41. When Herod ____ Jesus, he was exceeding glad. (Luke 23:8)
42. I will send you ____ the prophet before the . . . great and dreadful day. (Mal. 4:5)
44. The ____ soweth the word. (Mark 4:14)
47. A certain man, which had devils long time,

and ____ no clothes. (Luke 8:27)
49. Seeing a ____ fig tree by the road, He came to it, and found nothing. (Matt. 21:19 NASB)
50. Norse thunder god.
51. A foolish man, which built his house upon the ____. (Matt. 7:26)
52. Moses called Oshea the son of ____. (Num. 13:16)
53. I have made you a tester of metals and my people the ____. (Jer. 6:27 NIV)
54. We know not: he is of ____; ask him. (John 9:21)
56. Deliver the poor and needy: ____ them out of the hand of the wicked. (Ps. 82:4)

36

Across

1. Formic acid source.
4. The Nicolaitanes, which I ____ hate. (Rev. 2:6)
8. ____ told Jezebel all that Elijah had done. (1 Kings 19:1)
12. It was impossible for God to ____. (Heb. 6:18)
13. ____ the flock of God which is among you. (1 Peter 5:2)
14. It is a ____ thing that the king requireth. (Dan. 2:11)
15. The same anointing teacheth you of ____ things. (1 John 2:27)
16. Man's ____ is like that of the animals. (Eccles. 3:19 NIV)
17. Brought down with the trees of ____ unto the nether parts of the earth. (Ezek. 31:18)
18. An unfriendly man pursues ____ ends. (Prov. 18:1 NIV)
20. A woman that hath a familiar spirit at ____ - dor. (1 Sam. 28:7)
21. Who ____ thou that judgest another? (James 4:12)
22. I have filled him . . . with skill, ability and knowledge in all kinds of ____. (Exod. 31:3 NIV)
26. Between us and you a great ____ has been fixed. (Luke 16:26 NIV)
29. Pelt.
30. And shall ____ your flesh as it were fire. (James 5:3)
31. Philosophical element.
32. And when she saw Peter, she ____ up. (Acts 9:40)
33. Call me not Naomi, call me ____. (Ruth 1:20)
34. All that handle the ____, the mariners. (Ezek. 27:29)
35. To ____, that God was in Christ. (2 Cor. 5:19)
36. Let him take the ____ of life freely. (Rev. 22:17)
37. I ____ not Jerusalem above my chief joy. (Ps. 137:6)
39. The Valley of Siddim was full of ____ pits. (Gen. 14:10 NIV)
40. Ye are a chosen generation, a royal priesthood, ____ holy nation, a peculiar people. (1 Peter 2:9)
41. Be ____ to maintain good works. (Titus 3:8)

45. The Lord said unto Cain, Where is ____ thy brother? (Gen. 4:9)
48. Settle down and ____ the bread they eat. (2 Thess. 3:12 NIV)
49. (For she died) that she called his name Ben-____. (Gen. 35:18)
50. The governor took Jesus into the common ____. (Matt. 27:27)
51. *African Queen* scriptwriter.
52. Lod, and ____, the valley of craftsmen. (Neh. 11:35)
53. He took them up in his ____, put his hands upon them, and blessed them. (Mark 10:16)
54. When ye ____, ye may understand my knowledge. (Eph. 3:4)
55. With silver, iron, ____, and lead, they traded in thy fairs. (Ezek. 27:12)

Down

1. ____, my lord, I beseech thee. (Num. 12:11)
2. All the depths of the ____ will dry up. (Zech. 10:11 NIV)
3. What I ____ you in darkness, that speak ye. (Matt. 10:27)
4. Her husband has the right to ____ or to annul any vow. (Num. 30:13 GNB)
5. He that is unjust in the ____ is unjust. (Luke 16:10)
6. ____, which was the son of Adam. (Luke 3:38)
7. Lyric poem.
8. Like men condemned to die in the ____. (1 Cor. 4:9 NIV)
9. Was not found, because God ____ translated him. (Heb. 11:5)
10. ____ ye not then partial in yourselves? (James 2:4)
11. Called his name ____ -ammi. (Gen. 19:38)
19. Hold ____ the form of sound words. (2 Tim. 1:13)
20. They do alway ____ in their heart. (Heb. 3:10)
22. If thou wert ____ out of the olive tree which is wild. (Rom. 11:24)
23. How could your servant, a mere dog, accomplish such a ____. (2 Kings 8:13 NIV)
24. There came forth two she bears out of the wood, and ____ forty and two children. (2 Kings 2:24)

25. The ____ of your god Remphan. (Acts 7:43)
26. I will ____ off from the top of his young twigs a tender one. (Ezek. 17:22)
27. Let every man be swift to ____, slow to speak. (James 1:19)
28. An half ____ of land, which a yoke of oxen might plow. (1 Sam. 14:14)
29. They are waxen ____, they shine. (Jer. 5:28)
32. ____, give me this water, that I thirst not. (John 4:15)
33. I liken you, my darling, to a ____. (Song of Sol. 1:9 NIV)
35. Maimed, or having a ____, or scurvy, or scabbed. (Lev. 22:22)
36. Noah, being ____ of God of things not seen as yet. (Heb. 11:7)
38. To his own master he stands or ____. (Rom. 14:4 NIV)

39. Pithon, and Melech, and ____, and Ahaz. (1 Chron. 8:35)
41. A ____ of every unclean and hateful bird. (Rev. 18:2)
42. Keep thy ____ when thou goest to the house of God. (Eccles. 5:1)
43. Bakbukiah and ____, their brethren, were over against them. (Neh. 12:9)
44. Your adversary the devil, as a roaring ____. (1 Peter 5:8)
45. ____, she is broken that was the gates of the people. (Ezek. 26:2)
46. A false prophet, a Jew, whose name was ____ -Jesus. (Acts 13:6)
47. Shade tree.
48. That which ye have spoken in the ____ in closets. (Luke 12:3)

37

Across

1. I will give to everyone according to what he ____ done. (Rev. 22:13 NIV)
4. They are like grass which sprouts ____. (Ps. 90:5 NASB)
8. Gideon said, ____, O Lord God! (Judg. 6:22)
12. "Pay back what you ____ me!" he demanded. (Matt. 18:28 NIV)
13. Eloi, Eloi, ____ sabachthani? (Mark 15:34)
14. The law is not going to be lost to the priest, nor counsel to the ____. (Jer. 18:18 NASB)
15. ____ ye the words which were spoken. (Jude 17)
17. "Is that your own ____," Jesus asked. (John 18:34 NIV)
18. Samoan warrior.
19. To ____ them that were under the law. (Gal. 4:5)
21. The golden pot that had manna, and ____ rod. (Heb. 9:4)
24. Wrath.
25. ____ Bartimaeus, the son of Timaeus. (Mark 10:46)
26. ____ is unto me, if I preach not the gospel! (1 Cor. 9:16)
27. Supposing to ____ affliction to my bonds. (Phil. 1:16)
30. To have gained this harm and ____. (Acts 27:21)
31. There is a woman that hath a familiar spirit at En-____. (1 Sam. 28:7)
32. Threesome.
33. Abraham set seven ____ lambs of the flock by themselves. (Gen. 21:28)
34. Behold, a beam is in thine ____ eye. (Matt. 7:4)
35. I will never ____ thee, nor forsake thee. (Heb. 13:5)
36. Seek those things which ____ above. (Col. 3:1)
37. ____ the path of thy feet, and let all thy ways be established. (Prov. 4:26)
38. Elijah went up to the top of ____. (1 Kings 18:42)
41. Emmet.
42. I saw as it were ____ ____ of glass. (Rev. 15:2)

43. Let your ____ be turned to mourning. (James 4:9)
48. If thy father at all ____ me, then say. (1 Sam. 20:6)
49. Or ____ believe me for the very works' sake. (John 14:11)
50. ____ the son of Ikkesh the Tekoite. (2 Sam. 23:26)
51. The man who has doubts is condemned if he ____. (Rom. 14:23 NIV)
52. He that despised Moses' law ____ without mercy. (Heb. 10:28)
53. Will men take a ____ of it to hang any vessel? (Ezek. 15:3)

Down

1. Aaron thy brother died in mount ____. (Deut. 32:50)
2. Stand in ____, and sin not. (Ps. 4:4)
3. ____, which was the son of Noe. (Luke 3:36)
4. And I said, I see a rod of an ____ tree. (Jer. 1:11)
5. Father of Barnabas.
6. Uncle (Scottish).
7. Every battle of the ____ is with confused noise. (Isa. 9:5)
8. Some are already turned ____ after Satan. (1 Tim. 5:15)
9. Ye ____ men with burdens grievous to be borne. (Luke 11:46)
10. Askew.
11. Now the coat was without ____, woven from the top. (John 19:23)
16. Certain jackets.
20. Sooner.
21. Ever learning, and never ____ to come to the knowledge of the truth. (2 Tim. 3:7)
22. The city shall be low in ____ ____ place. (Isa. 32:19)
23. The dead in Christ shall ____ first. (1 Thess. 4:16)
26. A brother offended is harder to be ____. (Prov. 18:19)
27. ____ the Canaanite, which dwelt in the south. (Num. 33:40)
28. Headfirst leap.
29. If thou judge the law, thou art not a ____ of the law. (James 4:11)

31. Lot ____ in the cities of the plain. (Gen. 13:12)
32. Abraham gave the ____ of the spoils. (Heb. 7:4)
34. Iron is taken from the earth, and copper is smelted from ____. (Job 28:2 NIV)
35. I have ____ for thy salvation, O Lord. (Ps. 119:174)
36. The dust hardens into ____ ____. (Job 38:38 NASB)
37. ____ and wonder! Blind yourselves and be blind. (Isa. 29:9 NKJV)
38. Before they ____ together, she was found with child of the Holy Ghost. (Matt. 1:18)

39. The churches of ____ salute you. (1 Cor. 16:19)
40. That they may ____ from their labours. (Rev. 14:13)
44. Arab name.
45. That he may dip the ____ of his finger in water, and cool my tongue. (Luke 16:24)
46. Of ____, the family of the Erites. (Num. 26:16)
47. He saw Jesus afar off, he ____ and worshipped him. (Mark 5:6)

38

Across

1. Although you wash yourself with ____. (Jer. 2:22 NIV)
5. He was strong as the ____; yet I destroyed his fruit. (Amos 2:9)
9. Blessed art thou, Simon ____ -jona. (Matt. 16:17)
12. Whereas ____ saith, We are impoverished. (Mal. 1:4)
13. These men are full of new ____. (Acts 2:13)
14. Hath Satan filled thine heart to ____? (Acts 5:3)
15. A leader and ____ to the people. (Isa. 55:4)
17. Be sober, and hope to the ____ for the grace. (1 Peter 1:13)
18. The cloke that I left at ____ with Carpus. (2 Tim. 4:13)
19. Therefore shalt thou plant pleasant plants, and shalt set it with strange ____. (Isa. 17:10)
21. As a ____ doth gather her brood under her wings. (Luke 13:34)
23. Rents.
26. The ____ commandment is the word. (1 John 2:7)
29. They think it strange that ye ____ not with them. (1 Peter 4:4)
31. He that is holy, let him be holy ____. (Rev. 22:11)
32. Those members of the body, which we ____ less honorable. (1 Cor. 12:23 NASB)
34. ____ yet that he should offer himself often. (Heb. 9:25)
36. Celebes ox.
37. It is not for you to know the times or ____ the Father has set. (Acts 1:7 NIV)
39. ____ sent Joram his son unto king David. (2 Sam. 8:10)
41. Swindle.
42. I will give you thirty ____ and thirty change of garments. (Judg. 14:12)
44. Out of whose womb came the ____? (Job 38:29)
46. My ____ shall Tychicus declare unto you. (Col. 4:7)
48. He shall not approach: a blind man, or ____ ____. (Lev. 21:18)
52. ____ ye not what the scripture saith of Elias? (Rom. 11:2)
54. Jesus was born in ____ of Judea. (Matt. 2:1)
56. Abraham set seven ____ lambs of the flock. (Gen. 21:28)
57. Islands off Timor.
58. Moses set out with Joshua his ____. (Exod. 24:13 NIV)
59. Christ maketh thee whole: arise, and make thy ____. (Acts 9:34)
60. Mahli, and ____, and Jeremoth, three. (1 Chron. 23:23)
61. Being not a forgetful hearer, but a ____ of the work. (James 1:25)

Down

1. There rose up certain of the ____ of the Pharisees. (Acts 15:5)
2. "By this time there is a bad ____." (John 11:39 NIV)
3. Major- ____.
4. The sun went down when they were come to the hill of ____. (2 Sam. 2:24)
5. Washed us from our sins in his ____ blood. (Rev. 1:5)
6. Assists.
7. Bell's toll.
8. Around the Temple, was a ____ of small rooms. (Ezek. 41:5 GNB)
9. That ye should inherit a ____. (1 Peter 3:9)
10. Riblah on the east side of ____. (Num. 34:11)
11. For the sky is ____ and lowring. (Matt. 16:3)
16. Anna, a prophetess, the daughter of Phanuel, of the tribe of ____. (Luke 2:36)
20. Cloth strip, India.
22. Joshua the son of ____ was full of the spirit. (Deut. 34:9)
24. ____, lama sabachthani? (Mark 15:34)
25. They crowd around me and ____ my face. (Job 16:10 GNB)
26. Betting percentages.
27. Dinah the daughter of ____. (Gen. 34:1)
28. The flock ____ me, and I grew weary. (Zech. 11:8 NIV)
30. Having faithful children ____ accused of riot. (Titus 1:6)
33. Bringeth forth herbs ____ for them by whom it is dressed. (Heb. 6:7)

35. Isaac dwelt by the well Lahai- ____. (Gen. 25:11)
38. I will make Rabbah a ____ for camels. (Ezek. 25:5)
40. Compound suffix.
43. Spirited horse.
45. Shuthelah his son, and Ezer, and ____. (1 Chron. 7:21)
47. Diminutive suffix.
49. ____ went before the ark. (2 Sam. 6:4)
50. In the first year of Darius the ____. (Dan. 11:1)
51. Cuchulain's wife.
52. Whose trust shall be a spider's ____. (Job 8:14)
53. ____ no man any thing, but to love one another. (Rom. 13:8)
55. Jesus saith unto ____, Woman, what have I to do with thee? (John 2:4)

39

Across

1. ____, and Dumah, and Eshean. (Josh. 15:52)
5. There were false prophets also among ____ people. (2 Peter 2:1)
8. Grape juice.
12. He set it up in the plain of ____. (Dan. 3:1)
13. There be quick ____ flesh in the rising. (Lev. 13:10)
14. He called the name of the well ____. (Gen. 26:20)
15. But ye have made it ____ ____ of thieves. (Luke 19:46)
16. Direction: Jerusalem to Jericho.
17. Abdiel, the son of ____, chief of the house. (1 Chron. 5:15)
18. I know not the ____ of the voice. (1 Cor. 14:11)
20. Seek him that maketh the seven stars and ____. (Amos 5:8)
21. And have seen the ____ of the Lord. (James 5:11)
22. Speak not evil ____ of another. (James 4:11)
23. Take my yoke upon you, and ____ of me. (Matt. 11:29)
26. Ye are my ____, if ye do whatsoever I command. (John 15:14)
30. Uzzi and Uzziel, and Jerimoth, and ____. (1 Chron. 7:7)
31. Deliver thyself as a ____ from the hand of the hunter. (Prov. 6:5)
32. The children of Lod, Hadid, and ____. (Ezra 2:33)
33. The Lord knoweth how to ____ the godly out of temptations. (2 Peter 2:9)
36. I am the ____ which came down from heaven. (John 6:41)
38. Be not, as the hypocrites, of a ____ countenance. (Matt. 6:16)
39. Taking with them the ____ for divination. (Num. 22:7 NIV)
40. The same ____ subtilly with our kindred. (Acts 7:19)
43. ____ begat Sisamai. (1 Chron. 2:40)
47. Zophah, and ____, and Shelesh, and Amal. (1 Chron. 7:35)
48. Commotion.
49. Behold a ____ horse. (Rev. 6:8)
50. Ezekias begat Manasses; and Manasses begat ____. (Matt. 1:10)
51. He arose, and rebuked the winds and the ____. (Matt. 8:26)
52. Of ____, the family of the Eranites. (Num. 26:36)
53. It is neither fit for the ____, nor yet for the dunghill. (Luke 14:35)
54. Go to the ____, thou sluggard; consider her ways. (Prov. 6:6)
55. The sons of Zerah; Zimri, and Ethan, and Heman, and Calcol, and ____. (1 Chron. 2:6)

Down

1. ____ was not deceived, but the woman. (1 Tim. 2:14)
2. Though I be ____ in speech, yet not in knowledge. (2 Cor. 11:6)
3. And drove all from the temple ____. (John 2:15 NIV)
4. Lift ye up a ____ upon the high mountain. (Isa. 13:2)
5. Direction.
6. On these two commandments ____ all the law and the prophets. (Matt. 22:40)
7. He must bring two male lambs and one ____ lamb a year old. (Lev. 14:10 NIV)
8. Let the brother of low ____ rejoice. (James 1:9)
9. Jimnah, and Ishuah, and ____, and Beriah. (Gen. 46:17)
10. The sons of Merari by Jaaziah; ____, and Shoham. (1 Chron. 24:27)
11. Camel's hair, and with a girdle of a ____. (Mark 1:6)
19. There was no room for them in the ____. (Luke 2:7)
20. She called his name Ben-____ but his father called him Benjamin. (Gen. 35:18)
22. He searches the farthest recesses for ____ in the blackest darkness. (Job 28:3 NIV)
23. A chest, and bored a hole in the ____ of it. (2 Kings 12:9)
24. Sir, come down ____ my child die. (John 4:49)
25. To give physical or emotional pain.
26. And ____ thy pleasure they are and were created. (Rev. 4:11)
27. Sem, which was the son of ____. (Luke 3:36)
28. Deoxyribonucleic acid.

29. Jacco ____ pottage, and Esau came from the field. (Gen. 25:29)
31. A great ____ dragon, having seven heads. (Rev. 12:3)
34. They knew that the ____ was called Melita. (Acts 28:1)
35. When anyone went to a wine ____ to draw fifty measures. (Hag. 2:16 NIV)
36. For the ____ that is in the land of Assyria. (Isa. 7:18)
37. Behold, the hire of the labourers who have ____. (James 5:4)
39. Threw it there, and made the iron ____. (2 Kings 6:6 NIV)

40. Is gone down in the sun ____ of Ahaz, ten degrees. (Isa. 38:8)
41. Woman's name.
42. Heareth the word, and ____ with joy receiveth it. (Matt. 13:20)
43. The Lord God planted a garden eastward in ____. (Gen. 2:8)
44. ____ obeyed Abraham, calling him lord. (1 Peter 3:6)
45. Winglike.
46. Where are the gods of Sepharvaim, ____, and Ivah? (2 Kings 18:34)
48. Roboam begat Abia; and Abia begat ____. (Matt. 1:7)

40

Across

1. He burned the bones of the king of Edom into ____. (Amos 2:1)
5. Like ____, whom the king of Babylon roasted in the fire. (Jer. 29:22)
9. ____ thee two tables of stone like unto the first. (Deut. 10:1)
12. He made a whip out of cords, and drove all from the temple ____. (John 2:15 NIV)
13. Beside that which cometh of the ____ of his patrimony. (Deut. 18:8)
14. The serpent beguiled ____ through subtilty. (2 Cor. 11:3)
15. There was none that moved the ____, or opened the mouth, or peeped. (Isa. 10:14)
16. Why do the nations rage and the peoples ____ in vain? (Acts 4:25 NIV)
17. Behold a man riding upon a ____ horse. (Zech. 1:8)
18. A woman that hath a familiar spirit at ____-dor. (1 Sam. 28:7)
20. As if I would terrify you by ____. (2 Cor. 10:9)
22. I ____ thee, because thou art an austere man. (Luke 19:21)
26. We ____ that they could not enter in because of unbelief. (Heb. 3:19)
27. Education degree.
28. He brake the withs, as a thread of ____ is broken. (Judg. 16:9)
30. In the wall of the house he made narrowed ____. (1 Kings 6:6)
34. Eli, Eli, ____ sabachthani? (Matt. 27:46)
36. First the blade, then the ____. (Mark 4:28)
38. Can the rush grow up without ____? (Job 8:11)
39. Every branch that does bear fruit he ____ clean. (John 15:2 NIV)
41. We ____ our bread with the peril of our lives. (Lam. 5:9)
43. Joshua the son of ____, the servant of Moses. (Num. 11:28)
44. See thou hurt not the ____ and the wine. (Rev. 6:6)
46. Thou shalt be ____, because thy seat will be empty. (1 Sam. 20:18)
48. The fingers of a human hand appeared and wrote on the ____ of the wall. (Dan. 5:5 NIV)

52. Father of lights, with whom is ____ variableness. (James 1:17)
53. All that handle the ____, the mariners. (Ezek. 27:29)
54. Cobra genus.
56. The Pharisees began to ____ him vehemently. (Luke 11:53)
60. (For she died) that she called him name Ben-____. (Gen. 35:18)
61. The high places also of ____, the sin of Israel. (Hos. 10:8)
62. Punish the men that are settled on their ____. (Zeph. 1:12)
63. Silly women laden with sins, ____ away with divers lusts. (2 Tim. 3:6)
64. Suffer us to go away into the ____ of swine. (Matt. 8:31)
65. The ____ shall drink of the wine of the wrath. (Rev. 14:10)

Down

1. Sin is the transgression of the ____. (1 John 3:4)
2. Fifth son of Bela.
3. Honour all ____. Love the brotherhood. (1 Peter 2:17)
4. Who is going to harm you if you are ____ to do good? (1 Peter 3:13 NIV)
5. The sucking child shall play on the hole of the ____. (Isa. 11:8)
6. Pilate entered into the judgment ____ again. (John 18:33)
7. Brought a mixture of myrrh and ____. (John 19:39)
8. It had been ____ for them not to have known the way of righteousness. (2 Peter 2:21)
9. ____ have we no continuing city. (Heb. 13:14)
10. He that doeth the will of God abideth for ____. (1 John 2:17)
11. Marries.
19. As the fishes that are taken in an evil ____. (Eccles. 9:12)
21. The Nile will ____ with frogs. (Exod. 8:3 NIV)
22. She ____ in her body that she was healed. (Mark 5:29)
23. And spread his tent beyond the tower of ____. (Gen. 35:21)
24. Say ye unto your brethren, ____. (Hos. 2:1)

25. Naphtali is a ____ set free. (Gen. 49:21 NIV)
29. Every one that passeth by her shall hiss, and ____ his hand. (Zeph. 2:15)
31. Her ____ have reached unto heaven, and God hath remembered. (Rev. 18:5)
32. This is the ____ God, and eternal life. (1 John 5:20)
33. God shall ____ them strong delusion. (2 Thess. 2:11)
35. Mattathias, which was the son of ____. (Luke 3:25)
37. Elihu the son of Barachel the Buzite, of the kindred of ____. (Job 32:2)
40. He called the name of it ____. (Gen. 26:21)
42. Purge away thy dross, and take away all thy ____. (Isa. 1:25)

45. I will never ____ thee, nor forsake thee. (Heb. 13:5)
47. Cannot cease from sin; beguiling unstable ____. (2 Peter 2:14)
48. Go, wash in the ____ of Siloam. (John 9:7)
49. Narrow road.
50. It goes through ____ places seeking rest. (Matt. 12:43 NIV)
51. Whale oil cask.
55. Be not carried about with divers ____ strange doctrines. (Heb. 13:9)
57. Tumeric.
58. The way a ____ cutter engraves a seal. (Exod. 28:11 NIV)
59. Direction: Emmaus to Jerusalem.

41

Across

1. Smote them, until they came under Beth-____. (1 Sam. 7:11)
4. A certain man had a fig ____ planted in his vineyard. (Luke 13:6)
8. Whosoever denieth the Son, the ____ hath not the Father. (1 John 2:23)
12. Ben-____ but his father called him Benjamin. (Gen. 35:18)
13. How shall they ____ without a preacher? (Rom. 10:14)
14. Of the tribe of Issachar, ____ the son of Joseph. (Num. 13:7)
15. Lod, and ____, the valley of craftsmen. (Neh. 11:35)
16. ____ it, even to the foundation. (Ps. 137:7)
17. Middle (comb. form).
18. Ahaziah fell down through a ____. (2 Kings 1:2)
20. ____, in her mouth was an olive leaf. (Gen. 8:11)
21. German I.
22. ____ therefore to all their dues. (Rom. 13:7)
26. Who maketh his angels spirits, and his ministers a ____ of fire. (Heb. 1:7)
29. If a man is lazy, the rafters ____. (Eccles. 10:18 NIV)
30. The appointed barley and the ____ in their place. (Isa. 28:25)
31. Who will ____ Ahab king of Israel into attacking? (2 Chron. 18:19 NIV)
32. All his substance, which he had ____ in the land of Canaan. (Gen. 36:6)
33. Settle down and ____ the bread they eat. (2 Thess. 3:12 NIV)
34. I ____ no pleasant bread. (Dan. 10:3)
35. Worshipped, leaning upon the ____ of his staff. (Heb. 11:21)
36. Confined.
37. Mocked.
39. ____ thou the King of the Jews? (Matt. 27:11)
40. Let him ask ____ faith, nothing wavering. (James 1:6)
41. They delivered the ____. (Acts 15:30)
45. The children of Ezer are these; Bilhan, and Zaavan, and ____. (Gen. 36:27)
48. The last ____ was made a quickening spirit. (1 Cor. 15:45)
49. I will ____ you out of their bondage. (Exod. 6:6)
50. No man could learn that ____ but the hundred and forty and four thousand. (Rev. 14:3)
51. The camel, and the ____, and the coney. (Deut. 14:7)
52. He casteth forth his ____ like morsels. (Ps. 147:17)
53. Make sure that nobody ____ back wrong for wrong. (1 Thess. 5:15 NIV)
54. Many of them also which used curious ____ brought their books together. (Acts 19:19)
55. Out of Zebulun they that handle the ____ of the writer. (Judg. 5:14)

Down

1. Dip the tip of his finger in water, and ____ my tongue. (Luke 16:24)
2. ____, a prophetess, the daughter of Phanuel. (Luke 2:36)
3. They count it pleasure to ____ in the day time. (2 Peter 2:13)
4. For this thing I besought the Lord ____. (2 Cor. 12:8)
5. ____ hither thy finger, and behold my hands. (John 20:27)
6. Take thine ____, eat, drink, and be merry. (Luke 12:19)
7. How long will it be ____ thou be quiet? (Jer. 47:6)
8. Call for ____, whose surname is Peter. (Acts 11:13)
9. Delivered of a child when she was past ____. (Heb. 11:11)
10. Will they not say that ye are ____? (1 Cor. 14:23)
11. Samuel feared to shew ____ the vision. (1 Sam. 3:15)
19. And in the process of ____ it came to pass. (Gen. 4:3)
20. Make bare the ____, uncover the thigh. (Isa. 47:2)
22. The weasel, the ____, any kind of great lizard. (Lev. 11:29 NIV)
23. Unto their net, and burn incense unto their ____. (Hab. 1:16)
24. Ireland.
25. ____ your heart, and not your garments. (Joel 2:13)

Crossword grid with numbered cells: 1, 2, 3, 4, 5, 6, 7, 8, 9, 10, 11, 12, 13, 14, 15, 16, 17, 18, 19, 20, 21, 22, 23, 24, 25, 26, 27, 28, 29, 30, 31, 32, 33, 34, 35, 36, 37, 38, 39, 40, 41, 42, 43, 44, 45, 46, 47, 48, 49, 50, 51, 52, 53, 54, 55

26. With a great shout, that the wall fell down ____. (Josh. 6:20)

27. Also with the ____ I will praise you. (Ps. 71:22 NKJV)

28. He has brought Greeks into the temple ____. (Acts 21:28 NIV)

29. After the ____ Satan entered into him. (John 13:27)

32. He that layeth up treasure for himself, and is not rich toward ____. (Luke 12:21)

33. This man welcomes sinners and ____ with them. (Luke 15:2 NIV)

35. Were there not ____ cleansed? (Luke 17:17)

36. Not withal to signify the ____ laid against him. (Acts 25:27)

38. No one ____ or shouts in the vineyards. (Isa. 16:10 NIV)

39. Wherefore lay ____ all filthiness and superfluity. (James 1:21)

41. Israel journeyed, and spread his tent beyond the tower of ____. (Gen. 35:21)

42. Protect me from men of violence who plan to ____ my feet. (Ps. 140:4 NIV)

43. All the dust of the land became ____. (Exod. 8:17)

44. He will make her wilderness like ____. (Isa. 51:3)

45. The . . . child shall play on the hole of the ____. (Isa. 11:8)

46. The Chaldeans, Pekod, and Shoa, and ____. (Ezek. 23:23)

47. No man hath seen God at ____ time. (1 John 4:12)

48. Saith, ____, I am warm, I have seen the fire. (Isa. 44:16)

87

42

Across

1. He that eateth of their ____ dieth. (Isa. 59:5)
5. They that are ____ of them are destroyed. (Isa. 9:16)
8. Write in it with a man's pen concerning Maher-shalal-____ -baz. (Isa. 8:1)
12. And use an abundance of ____, the stain of your guilt is still before me. (Jer. 2:22 NIV)
13. They ____ in vision, they stumble in judgment. (Isa. 28:7)
14. Center of the ____ that belongs to the prince. (Ezek. 48:22 NIV)
15. Taro root.
16. Pochereth of Zebaim, the children of ____. (Ezra 2:57)
17. Saying, ____ this, I pray thee: and he saith, I am not learned. (Isa. 29:12)
18. She named the child ____. (1 Sam. 4:21)
21. No longer fresh.
24. The fowls of heaven made their ____ in his boughs. (Ezek. 31:6)
28. The Valley of Siddim was full of ____ pits. (Gen. 14:10 NIV)
29. Seeing I have ____ my children, and am desolate. (Isa. 49:21)
33. I will fasten him as a ____ in a sure place. (Isa. 22:23)
34. His mother's name also was ____, the daughter of Zachariah. (2 Kings 18:2)
35. Isaac dwelt by the well ____ -roi. (Gen. 25:11)
37. German name meaning industrious.
38. ____ a mocker, and the simple will learn. (Prov. 19:25 NIV)
40. I will give free ____ to my complaint. (Job 10:1 NIV)
41. Naval abbreviation.
42. Malodorous.
44. Pilate wrote a ____, and put it on the cross. (John 19:19)
46. The _____, and his Spirit, hath sent me. (Isa. 48:16)
50. Shout, so that the earth ____ again. (1 Sam. 4:5)
53. ____ the son of Ikkesh the Tekoite. (1 Chron. 27:9)
54. The waste places of the fat ____ shall strangers eat. (Isa. 5:17)

58. "Is that your own ____," Jesus asked. (John 18:34 NIV)
59. I ____ not in the assembly of the mockers. (Jer. 15:17)
60. In his ____ and in his pity he redeemed them. (Isa. 63:9)
61. The dew out of the fleece, a ____ full of water. (Judg. 6:38)
62. The poor man had nothing, save one little ____. (2 Sam. 12:3)
63. Let me have some of that red ____! (Gen. 25:30 NIV)

Down

1. Direction: Bethlehem to Herodium.
2. He that doeth good is of ____. (3 John 11)
3. A troop cometh: and she called his name ____. (Gen. 30:11)
4. The ____ of the poor is in your houses. (Isa. 3:14)
5. Like Rachel and like ____, which two did build the house of Israel. (Ruth 4:11)
6. German name meaning power.
7. Drop.
8. Yea, I would ____ myself in sorrow. (Job 6:10)
9. Thy counsels of old ____ faithfulness and truth. (Isa. 25:1)
10. The burden of the desert of the ____. (Isa. 21:1)
11. Behold, for peace I ____ great bitterness. (Isa. 38:17)
19. Jeremiah was put into a vaulted ____. (Jer. 37:16 NIV)
20. The young lion roaring ____ his prey. (Isa. 31:4)
21. The fitches are beaten out with a ____. (Isa. 28:27)
22. Now go, write it before them in a ____. (Isa. 30:8)
23. There may be ____ ____ among the people. (Matt. 26:5 NIV)
25. Aaron the ____ of the Lord. (Ps. 106:16)
26. Chedorlaomer king of Elam, and ____ king of nations. (Gen. 14:1)
27. Is Israel a servant? is he a homeborn ____? (Jer. 2:14)
30. Paddle.

88

A crossword grid numbered 1–63.

31. And ____ being desolate shall sit upon the ground. (Isa. 3:26)
32. Oriental porgy.
36. That which is crushed breaketh out ____ a viper. (Isa. 59:5)
39. Elijah went with Elisha from ____. (2 Kings 2:1)
43. The Lord will ____ this thing that he hath spoken. (Isa. 38:7)
45. And the ____ he shall utterly abolish. (Isa. 2:18)
47. Woe unto them that ____ up early in the morning. (Isa. 5:11)

48. Let the counsel of the Holy One of Israel ____ nigh. (Isa. 5:19)
49. Howl, O ____; cry, O city. (Isa. 14:31)
50. The ____, which the Lord God had taken from man, made he a woman. (Gen. 2:22)
51. Commotion.
52. The ____ wine is found in the cluster. (Isa. 65:8)
55. A bruised reed shall he ____ break. (Isa. 42:3)
56. Adam was first formed, then ____. (1 Tim. 2:13)
57. Woe to the women that ____ pillows. (Ezek. 13:18)

89

43

Across

1. They drive away the ____ of the fatherless. (Job 24:3)
4. Bind the ____ of thine head upon thee. (Ezek. 24:17)
8. Have they not ____? have they not divided the prey? (Judg. 5:30)
12. Animal constellation.
13. Medical study (abbrev.).
14. The sons of Lotan; ____, and Homam. (1 Chron. 1:39)
15. We should be holy ____ without blame before him. (Eph. 1:4)
16. The city of David, which is called ____. (Luke 2:4)
18. Delivered by riders mounted on fast horses from the royal ____. (Esther 8:10 GNB)
20. Hawaiian bird.
21. It will be fair weather: for the sky is ____. (Matt. 16:2)
22. The doctrine of ____, who taught Balac. (Rev. 2:14)
26. ____' husband was Abraham.
29. Confess that Jesus is the ____ of God. (1 John 4:15)
30. We receive the ____ reward of our deeds. (Luke 23:41)
31. Is any among you afflicted? let him ____. (James 5:13)
32. The ____ of the Lord will come as a thief. (2 Peter 3:10)
33. Evil (Latin).
34. Of ____, the family of the Erites. (Num. 26:16)
35. The ____ of truth shall be established. (Prov. 12:19)
36. ____ sought to destroy all the Jews. (Esther 3:6)
37. We have ____ all things, and have been consumed. (Jer. 44:18)
39. Blade.
40. Egyptian sun god.
41. If ____ were justified by works, he hath whereof to glory; but not before God. (Rom. 4:2)
45. The holy ____, descending out of heaven from God. (Rev. 21:10)
49. The heavens ____ the works of thine hands. (Heb. 1:10)
50. Give to drink unto one of these little ____ a cup of cold water. (Matt. 10:42)
51. Actual being.
52. They ____ the ship aground. (Acts 27:41)
53. Covet earnestly the ____ gifts. (1 Cor. 12:31)
54. Having foot digits.
55. Which of you with taking thought can ____ to his stature one cubit? (Luke 12:25)

Down

1. Gideon said, ____, O Lord God! (Judg. 6:22)
2. God hath ____ forth the Spirit of his Son. (Gal. 4:6)
3. Like vinegar poured on ____. (Prov. 25:20 NIV)
4. We should leave the word of God, and serve ____. (Acts 6:2)
5. Have ____ of mad men? (1 Sam. 21:15)
6. Five gold tumors and five gold ____. (1 Sam. 6:4 NIV)
7. Ordinal suffix.
8. In ____ who will give Thee thanks? (Ps. 6:5 NASB)
9. Exclamation of doubt.
10. How long will it be ____ they believe? (Num. 14:11)
11. How is the gold become ____! (Lam. 4:1)
17. The ____ which is lent to the Lord. (1 Sam. 2:20)
19. Though thou shouldest ____ a fool in a mortar. (Prov. 27:22)
22. A ____ for an harlot, and sold a girl for wine. (Joel 3:3)
23. Enoch also, the seventh from ____. (Jude 14)
24. Hall (German).
25. What ____ ye to weep and to break mine heart? (Acts 21:13)
26. They ____ out swords from their lips. (Ps. 59:7 NIV)
27. Irish exclamation.
28. The ____ descended, and the floods came. (Matt. 7:25)
29. The trees of the Lord are full of ____. (Ps. 104:16)
32. Have ye not read what David ____? (Matt. 12:3)
33. Call me not Naomi, call me ____. (Ruth 1:20)
35. Pastures.

36. The fire had not ____ their bodies. (Dan. 3:27 NIV)
38. We ____ in the living God, who is the Saviour of all men. (1 Tim. 4:10)
39. Extremely fat.
41. I ____ will keep thee from the hour of temptation. (Rev. 3:10)
42. Brought them unto Halah, and Habor, and ____. (1 Chron. 5:26)

43. ____ the Canaanite, which dwelt in the south. (Num. 33:40)
44. Brass to ____ the house of the Lord. (2 Chron. 24:12)
45. Ye have heard of the patience of ____. (James 5:11)
46. Direction: Nazareth to Tiberias.
47. Thing (Latin).
48. Of the age (abbrev.).

44

Across

1. The sons of Ram . . . were Maaz, and Jamin, and ____. (1 Chron. 2:27)
5. He planteth an ____, and the rain doth nourish it. (Isa. 44:14)
8. ____ is love, that we walk after his commandments. (2 John 6)
12. Those that were clean escaped from them who ____ in error. (2 Peter 2:18)
13. Greenland Eskimo.
14. Catholic tribunal.
15. Their ____ of pleasure is to carouse. (2 Peter 2:13 NIV)
16. Make bare the ____. (Isa. 47:2)
17. His ears are ____ unto prayers. (1 Peter 3:12)
18. Jesus had made an end of ____ his twelve disciples. (Matt. 11:1)
21. ____, it therefore in your hearts, not to meditate. (Luke 21:14)
24. In the first chariot were ____ horses. (Zech. 6:2)
25. The spirit of whoredoms hath caused them to ____. (Hos. 4:12)
26. Rejoicing of the hope firm unto the ____. (Heb. 3:6)
28. They gnashed on him with their ____. (Acts 7:54)
32. Journey.
34. Poetic contraction of "it is."
36. None.
37. A Prophet was beforetime called ____ ____ (1 Sam. 9:9)
39. James, he did ____ with the Gentiles. (Gal. 2:12)
41. ____, which was the son of Noe. (Luke 3:36)
42. Dance step.
44. If a serpent had ____ any man, when he beheld the serpent of brass, he lived. (Num. 21:9)
46. Saying, I ____ ____ my faults this day. (Gen. 41:9)
50. Worshipped God that sat on the throne, saying, ____; Alleluia. (Rev. 19:4)
51. Extinct bird.
52. Learn to maintain good words for necessary ____. (Titus 3:14)
56. They spread Absalom a ____ upon the top of the house. (2 Sam. 16:22)
57. Is (Latin).
58. A man plucked off his ____, and gave it to his neighbour. (Ruth 4:7)
59. Many of them also which used curious ____. (Acts 19:19)
60. ____-bosheth the son of Saul. (2 Sam. 2:8)]
61. The hour of trial . . . to ____ those who live on the earth. (Rev. 3:10 NIV)

Down

1. ____, the Lord's priest in Shiloh. (1 Sam. 14:3)
2. Thou never gavest me a ____. (Luke 15:29)
3. The serpent beguiled ____ through his subtilty. (2 Cor. 11:3)
4. Respond.
5. I was given a painful physical ____. (2 Cor. 12:7 GNB)
6. Shall come forth a rod out of the ____ of Jesse. (Isa. 11:1)
7. ____ bare Ishmael to Abram. (Gen. 16:16)
8. Jerusalem shall be ____ down of the Gentiles. (Luke 21:24)
9. American Indian tribe.
10. Bolivian Indian tribe.
11. At midnight Paul and Silas prayed, and ____ praises unto God. (Acts 16:25)
19. Bullfight cheer.
20. He is cast into a ____ by his own feet. (Job 18:8)
21. Shut him up, and ____ ____ seal upon him. (Rev. 20:3)
22. Greek Cupid.
23. Let God be ____, but every man a liar. (Rom. 3:4)
27. It is appointed unto men once to ____. (Heb. 9:27)
29. Lo, the star, which they saw in the ____. (Matt. 2:9)
30. Climbed up into a sycamore ____ to see him. (Luke 19:4)
31. When they had sung an ____, they went out into the mount of Olives. (Mark 14:26)
33. Rejoicing in heaven over one sinner who ____. (Luke 15:7 NIV)
35. Made a man every whit whole on the ____ day. (John 7:23)

1	2	3	4		5	6	7		8	9	10	11
12					13				14			
15					16				17			
			18	19				20				
21	22	23					24					
25				26		27		28		29	30	31
32			33		34		35		36			
37				38		39		40		41		
			42		43		44		45			
46	47	48				49						
50					51				52	53	54	55
56					57				58			
59					60				61			

38. The ____ which thou sawest having two horns. (Dan. 8:20)
40. Bind them continually upon thine heart, and ____ them about thy neck. (Prov. 6:21)
43. ____, which was the son of Joseph. (Luke 3:26)
45. Then come and put your ____ in my shadow. (Judg. 9:15)
46. Information.
47. Take a pot, and put an ____ full of manna therein. (Exod. 16:33)
48. The Lord hath ____ the kingdom of Israel. (1 Sam. 15:28)
49. Musci, plant of.
53. Elisabeth's full time came that ____ should be delivered. (Luke 1:57)
54. Greek dawn goddess.
55. Course of nature; and it is ____ on fire of hell. (James 3:6)

45

Across

1. Who is he that will ____ you, if ye be followers. (1 Peter 3:13)
5. Hebrew letter.
8. These shall stand upon mount ____ to curse. (Deut. 27:13)
12. ____ is Edom. (Gen. 36:8)
13. The two sons of ____, Hophni and Phinehas. (1 Sam. 1:3)
14. The rings of the ephod with a ____ of blue. (Exod. 28:28)
15. Judgeth according to every ____ work. (1 Peter 1:17)
16. Doer's suffix.
17. They shall turn away their ____ from the truth. (2 Tim. 4:4)
18. The book of the ____ of the kings of Media and Persia. (Esther 10:2)
21. People in Sardis who have not ____ their clothes. (Rev. 3:4 NIV)
24. Their word will ____ as doth a canker. (2 Tim. 2:17)
25. Saul the son of Kish, and ____ the son of Ner. (1 Chron. 26:28)
26. Doctrinal suffix.
27. Your fathers tempted me, proved me, and ____ my works. (Heb. 3:9)
30. Under the whole heaven He ____ it loose. (Job 37:3 NASB)
31. A . . . man lame from his mother's womb ____ carried. (Acts 3:2)
32. Reap; for the harvest of the earth is ____. (Rev. 14:15)
33. Why make ye this ____, and weep? (Mark 5:39)
34. The kingdom of heaven be likened unto ____ virgins. (Matt. 25:1)
35. The ____ are the children of the wicked one. (Matt. 13:38)
36. The sons of Benjamin were . . . Gera, and Naaman, ____, and Rosh. (Gen. 46:21)
37. When thou ____ a vow unto God, defer not. (Eccles. 5:4)
38. While the ____ tarried, they all slumbered. (Matt. 25:5)
42. Ladder step.
43. Jacob sojourned in the land of ____. (Ps. 105:23)

44. If a man ____ of this bread, he will live. (John 6:51 NIV)
48. To be (French).
49. Three (prefix).
50. John to the seven churches which are in ____. (Rev. 1:4)
51. Greek letters.
52. ____ once more I shake not the earth only. (Heb. 12:26)
53. When ____ shall say, Peace and safety; then sudden destruction cometh. (1 Thess. 5:3)

Down

1. And touched the ____ of his garment. (Matt. 9:20)
2. ____ had an army of men that bare targets. (2 Chron. 14:8)
3. He ____ before, and climbed up into a sycomore. (Luke 19:4)
4. What power in the ____ of his belly! (Job 40:16 NIV)
5. ____ sights will appear before your eyes. (Prov. 23:33 GNB)
6. I ____ will keep thee from the hour of temptation. (Rev. 3:10)
7. To bear ____ of the Light. (John 1:7)
8. If it were possible, they should deceive the very ____. (Matt. 24:24)
9. They taught my people to swear by ____. (Jer. 12:16)
10. An half ____ of land, which a yoke of oxen might plow. (1 Sam. 14:14)
11. The ____ is blessed of the better. (Heb. 7:7)
19. Let every woman have ____ own husband. (1 Cor. 7:2)
20. As he had said unto them, _____ he, they went backward. (John 18:6)
21. Heber, which was the son of ____. (Luke 3:35)
22. And Boaz begat ____ of Ruth. (Matt. 1:5)
23. Many false prophets are gone out ____ the world. (1 John 4:1)
26. Gaelic John.
27. Father.
28. Bringing gold, and silver, ivory, and ____. (1 Kings 10:22)
29. When ye see a cloud rise out of the ____. (Luke 12:54)

Crossword grid with numbered cells:

1	2	3	4		5	6	7		8	9	10	11
12					13				14			
15					16				17			
			18	19				20				
21	22	23					24					
25						26				27	28	29
30					31				32			
33				34				35				
			36				37					
38	39	40				41						
42					43				44	45	46	47
48					49				50			
51					52				53			

31. A stone is heavy, and the sand ____. (Prov. 27:3)

32. He won't accept boiled meat from you, only ____ ____. (1 Sam. 2:15 GNB)

34. I came not to call ____ righteous, but sinners. (Luke 5:32)

35. Such knowledge is ____ wonderful for me. (Ps. 139:6)

36. He which hath the sharp sword with two ____. (Rev. 2:12)

37. The dog is turned to his own ____ again. (2 Peter 2:22)

38. "Uncle Remus" rabbit.

39. ____ said, Intreat me not to leave thee. (Ruth 1:16)

40. Nested boxes.

41. It is a ____ thing that the king requireth. (Dan. 2:11)

45. Burn it in a wood fire on the ____ pile. (Lev. 4:12 NIV)

46. ____ the kine to the cart, and bring their calves. (1 Sam. 6:7)

47. Let no man ____ when he is tempted, I am tempted of God. (James 1:13)

95

46

Across

1. Will a lion ____ in the forest, when he hath no prey? (Amos 3:4)
5. A false prophet, a Jew, whose name was ____ -jesus. (Acts 13:6)
8. The cup was found in Benjamin's ____. (Gen. 44:12)
12. Monster.
13. What mean these seven ____ lambs? (Gen. 21:29)
14. Who will commit to your trust the ____ riches? (Luke 16:11)
15. And the ____ thereof for medicine. (Ezek. 47:12)
16. He that is without sin among you, ____ him first cast a stone. (John 8:7)
17. Let us labour therefore to enter into that ____. (Heb. 4:11)
18. O ____, it is not for kings to drink wine. (Prov. 31:4)
20. The Lord struck the child that ____ wife bare unto David. (2 Sam. 12:15)
22. Many will ____ to me in that day, Lord, Lord. (Matt. 7:22)
23. Aaron's ____ that budded. (Heb. 9:4)
24. I would not write with ____ and ink. (2 John 12)
27. The child ____ seven times, and the child opened his eyes. (2 Kings 4:35)
31. In the resurrection they neither marry, nor ____ given in marriage. (Matt. 22:30)
32. Poetic contraction.
33. The sons of Gad . . . Ezbon, ____, and Arodi, and Areli. (Gen. 46:16)
34. Portable protective case for a light.
37. There are ____ that bear record in heaven. (1 John 5:7)
39. I took the little book out of the angel's hand, and ____ it up. (Rev. 10:10)
40. All the hills once cultivated by the ____. (Isa. 7:25 NIV)
41. Then ____ said, Shoot. And he shot. (2 Kings 13:17)
44. Sewed fig leaves together, and made themselves ____. (Gen. 3:7)
48. The Angel which redeemed me from all evil, bless the ____. (Gen. 48:16)

49. The eyes of Israel were ____ for age. (Gen. 48:10)
51. Over the camels also was ____ the Ishmaelite. (1 Chron. 27:30)
52. Naphtali is ____ ____ set free. (Gen. 49:21 NIV)
53. Historical time period.
54. Then he went to the temple to give notice of the ____. (Acts 21:26 NIV)
55. Because thou wilt not leave my soul in ____. (Acts 2:27)
56. One ____ and filled a sponge full of vinegar. (Mark 15:36)
57. O fools, and ____ of heart to believe. (Luke 24:25)

Down

1. Who shall ____ us away the stone from the door. (Mark 16:3)
2. Pointed arch.
3. ____ begat Aminadab; and Aminadab begat Naasson. (Matt. 1:4)
4. ____ profane and old wives' fables. (1 Tim. 4:7)
5. Whose end is destruction, whose God is their ____. (Phil. 3:19)
6. Stand in ____, and sin not. (Ps. 4:4)
7. As a dog ____ to its vomit. (Prov. 26:11 NIV)
8. There are three things that are stately in their ____. (Prov. 30:29 NIV)
9. He measured the ____ on all four sides. (Ezek. 42:20 NIV)
10. ____ begat Nimrod: he began to be mighty. (1 Chron. 1:10)
11. Egyptian weights.
19. First the blade, then the ____. (Mark 4:28)
21. Asahel was as light of foot as a wild ____. (2 Sam. 2:18)
24. Friend.
25. Jephunneh, and Pispah, and ____. (1 Chron. 7:38)
26. Judah is written with a ____ of iron. (Jer. 17:1)
27. His Son cleanseth us from all ____. (1 John 1:7)
28. The fenced cities are Ziddim, ____, and Hammath. (Josh. 19:35)
29. Sooner.

30. Desire to ____, and death shall flee from them. (Rev. 9:6)
32. The ____ of grapes him that soweth seed. (Amos 9:13)
35. Dangling ornament.
36. Anglo-Saxon letter.
37. A tower, whose ____ may reach unto heaven. (Gen. 11:4)
38. When ____ birthday was kept, the daughter of Herodias danced. (Matt. 14:6)
40. ____ was fallen upon the bed whereon Esther was. (Esther 7:8)
41. Hoshea the son of ____ made a conspiracy. (2 Kings 15:30)

42. Ye lawyers! for ye ____ men with burdens grievous. (Luke 11:46)
43. Woe to the ____ shepherd that leaveth the flock! (Zech. 11:17)
45. And ____, and Abimael, and Sheba. (Gen. 10:28)
46. Climbing fern.
47. The commandment, deceived me, and by it ____ me. (Rom. 7:11)
50. ____ the son of Ikkesh the Tekoite. (1 Chron. 11:28)

47

Across

1. Sir, thou hast nothing to ____ with. (John 4:11)
5. Went to make war with the remnant of her ____. (Rev. 12:17)
9. ____ me, and deliver me from the hand of strange children. (Ps. 144:11)
12. Gaelic Ireland.
13. Or ____ believe me for the very works' sake. (John 14:11)
14. Sir, come down ____ my child die. (John 4:49)
15. My tears will pour out in a ____ stream. (Lam. 3:49 GNB)
17. Give an answer to every ____ that asketh you. (1 Peter 3:15)
18. We spend our years as a ____ that is told. (Ps. 90:9)
19. A friend of the world is the ____ of God. (James 4:4)
21. Where, then, are the ____ of divorce? (Isa. 50:1 GNB)
24. Percussion instrument.
25. They may ____ the doctrine of God our Saviour. (Titus 2:10)
26. They are ____ with the showers of the mountains. (Job 24:8)
27. There will I make the horn of David to ____. (Ps. 132:17)
30. Man's name.
31. He cannot ____, because he is born of God. (1 John 3:9)
32. Ye ____ sometimes darkness, but now are ye light. (Eph. 5:8)
33. The prophets that make my people ____. (Mic. 3:5)
34. Ye did ____ well; who did hinder you? (Gal. 5:7)
35. Blend.
36. See where thou hast not been ____ with. (Jer. 3:2)
38. Then is the offence of the cross ____. (Gal. 5:11)
39. Like men condemned to die in the ____. (1 Cor. 4:9 NIV)
41. The silver cord be loosed, or the golden ____ be broken. (Eccles. 12:6)
42. Do count them but dung, that I may ____ Christ. (Phil. 3:8)
43. Almost thou persuadest me to be a ____. (Acts 26:28)
48. ____ to your faith virtue. (2 Peter 1:5)
49. Indian mahogany.
50. When I looked, behold a ____ in the wall. (Ezek. 8:7)
51. ____ verily, their sound went into all the earth. (Rom. 10:18)
52. No one ____ a patch of unshrunk cloth on an old garment. (Mark 2:21 NIV)
53. Twelve day heathen feast.

Down

1. One of the twelve months (abbrev.).
2. The appointed barley and ____ in their place? (Isa. 28:25)
3. Brazilian parrot.
4. As for the ____ border, ye shall even have the great sea. (Num. 34:6)
5. She makes linen garments and ____ them. (Prov. 31:24 NIV)
6. Confederate General Robert ____ ____.
7. Nineteenth letter.
8. Was without in ____ places: and they came to him. (Mark 1:45)
9. The Lord ____ us and will bless us. (Ps. 115:12 NIV)
10. Duke Magdiel, duke ____: these be the dukes of Edom. (Gen. 36:43)
11. They know God; but in works they ____ him. (Titus 1:16)
16. You ____ wages, only to put them in a purse with holes in it. (Hag. 1:6 NIV)
20. Greek letter.
21. I looked, and behold a ____ horse. (Rev. 6:8)
22. Zebadiah, and Arad, and ____. (1 Chron. 8:15)
23. He who is kind to the ____ ____ to the Lord. (Prov. 19:17 NIV)
24. To make the cities of Judah desolate, and a ____ of dragons. (Jer. 10:22)
26. Thought to ____ them [fenced cities] for himself. (2 Chron. 32:2)
28. The Pharisees began to ____ him vehemently. (Luke 11:53)
29. Man shall be blessed in his ____. (James 1:25)

31. There shall be signs in the ____. (Luke 21:25)
32. Arise, get you up unto the ____ nation. (Jer. 49:31)
34. Responds.
35. Royal stables.
37. You should know how to possess his vessel ____ sanctification and honour. (1 Thess. 4:4)
38. He scattered the ____ of the money changers. (John 2:15 NIV)
39. Beware lest ye also, being led ____ with the error of the wicked, fall. (2 Peter 3:17)

40. We will ____ upon the swift. (Isa. 30:16)
41. Led him out of the city, and led him unto the ____ of the hill. (Luke 4:29)
44. The hills once cultivated by the ____. (Isa. 7:25 NIV)
45. Debt note.
46. ____ the law is fulfilled in one word. (Gal. 5:14)
47. Born.

48

Across

1. Reverse point.
5. No man was found worthy to open and to ____ the book. (Rev. 5:4)
9. ____ shall be a serpent by the way. (Gen. 49:17)
12. Double reeded instrument.
13. Rhine feeder.
14. How long shall it be then, ____ thou bid the people return? (2 Sam. 2:26)
15. A meat offering, and ____ ____ of oil. (Lev. 14:21)
16. Whatever ____ it is, in which any work is done, it must be put in water. (Lev. 11:32 NKJV)
17. And smote them, until they came under Beth-____. (1 Sam. 7:11)
18. ____ your ways and your actions. (Jer. 7:3 NIV)
20. ____ that man, and have no company with him. (2 Thess. 3:14)
22. ____ the kine to the cart. (1 Sam. 6:7)
23. ____ not thyself with oil. (2 Sam. 14:2)
26. The gospel which ____ preached of me is not after man. (Gal. 1:11)
29. The latter ____ is worse with them than the beginning. (2 Peter 2:20)
31. ____ the wicked from among the just. (Matt. 13:49)
32. Even in laughter the heart may ____. (Prov. 14:13 NIV)
34. Purge away thy dross. and take away all thy ____. (Isa. 1:25)
36. Whey.
37. Hole maker.
39. Petrol.
41. Dash their children, and ____ up their women with child. (2 Kings 8:12)
42. Balancing toy.
44. That he may dip the ____ of his finger in water. (Luke 16:24)
46. Dinah the daughter of ____. (Gen. 34:1)
47. The Lord struck the child that ____ wife bare. (2 Sam. 12:15)
51. The other I called Bands; and I ____ the flock. (Zech. 11:7)
53. The judge standeth before the ____. (James 5:9)
55. Before (Latin).
56. How much do you ____ my master? (Luke 16:5 NIV)
57. The churches of ____ salute you. (1 Cor. 16:19)
58. ____ your bread there and do your prophesying there. (Amos 7:12 NIV)
59. Bring thee a ____ heifer without spot. (Num. 19:2)
60. Death, and ____ followed with him. (Rev. 6:8)
61. They have ____ the blood of saints. (Rev. 16:6)

Down

1. The ____ out of the wood doth waste it. (Ps. 80:13)
2. He is ____ to succour them that are tempted. (Heb. 2:18)
3. I am not worthy that thou shouldest enter under my ____. (Luke 7:6)
4. Everyone who loves Him who ____ also loves him who is begotten. (1 John 5:1 NKJV)
5. Having food and ____ let us be therewith content. (1 Tim. 6:8)
6. I will give to ____ of the tree of life. (Rev. 2:7)
7. Like men condemned to die in the ____. (1 Cor. 4:9 NIV)
8. She has become a home for ____. (Rev. 18:2 NIV)
9. The deceived and the ____ are his. (Job 12:16)
10. Jephunneh, and Pispah, and ____. (1 Chron. 7:38)
11. Abner, the son of ____, Saul's uncle. (1 Sam. 14:50)
19. But the wheat and the ____ were not smitten. (Exod. 9:32)
21. And ____, part of potters' clay, and part of iron. (Dan. 2:41)
24. Salathiel, which was the son of ____. (Luke 3:27)
25. Let their table be made a snare, and a ____. (Rom. 11:9)
26. Lots (informal).
27. An half ____ of land, which a yoke of oxen might plow. (1 Sam. 14:14)
28. Who through faith are ____ by God's power. (1 Peter 1:5 NIV)

100

30. I cannot ____; to beg I am ashamed. (Luke 16:3)
33. I am the Lord, and there is none ____. (Isa. 45:6)
35. His eye was not dim, nor his ____ force abated. (Deut. 34:7)
38. ____ the father of Mareshah. (1 Chron. 4:21)
40. ____, if thou have borne him hence, tell me where. (John 20:15)
43. The first beast, ____ deadly wound was healed. (Rev. 13:12)
45. Mine heart shall sound for Moab like ____. (Jer. 48:36)

48. The sons of Ulla; ____, and Haniel, and Rezia. (1 Chron. 7:39)
49. The ____, because he cheweth the cud. (Lev. 11:6)
50. Make merry, and shall ____ gifts one to another. (Rev. 11:10)
51. ____ the prophecy came not in old time by the will of man. (2 Peter 1:21)
52. He must bring two male lambs and one ____ lamb a year old. (Lev. 14:10 NIV)
54. Give us of your ____; for our lamps are gone out. (Matt. 25:8)

49

Across

1. The commandment, deceived me, and by it ____ me. (Rom. 7:11)
5. Lest at any time we should let them ____. (Heb. 2:1)
9. The people of God: which ____ not obtained mercy. (2 Peter 2:10)
12. I looked, and behold a ____ horse. (Rev. 6:8)
13. Lest that which is ____ be turned out of the way. (Heb. 12:13)
14. Therefore said his parents, He is of ____; ask him. (John 9:23)
15. Thy King cometh, sitting on an ____ colt. (John 12:15)
16. I went . . . to ____ and beat those who believed in you. (Acts 22:19 NIV)
18. An hiding place from the wind, and a covert from ____. (Isa. 32:2)
20. Direction: Gaza to Jerusalem.
21. He ____ night, and smote the Edomites. (2 Kings 8:21)
25. We his servants will ____ rebuilding. (Neh. 2:20 NIV)
28. Thought to ____ them [fenced cities] for himself. (2 Chron. 32:1)
29. As it was in the days of ____, so shall it be. (Luke 17:26)
30. For he hath ____, and he will heal us. (Hos. 6:1)
31. Honey.
32. Thou art Simon the son of ____. (John 1:42)
33. By grace ____ ye saved through faith. (Eph. 2:8)
34. Take thou unto thee an iron ____. (Ezek. 4:3)
35. Asker of riddles.
36. Warned of God in a dream that they should not ____ to Herod. (Matt. 2:12)
38. Hadadezer had wars with ____. (2 Sam. 8:10)
39. A wise man's heart ____ both time and judgment. (Eccles. 8:5)
44. Filthy dreamers defile the flesh, despise ____. (Jude 8)
47. Sibbecai the Hushathite, ____ the Ahohite. (1 Chron. 11:29)
48. Whose names ____ not written in the book of life. (Rev. 13:8)
49. They cast their garments upon the ____. (Luke 19:35)
50. Knot, fiber.
51. At thy word I will let down the ____. (Luke 5:5)
52. For salvation unto the ____ of the earth. (Acts 13:47)
53. Four fluid ounces.

Down

1. He ____ on the ground, and made clay of the spittle. (John 9:6)
2. You will be protected from the ____ of the tongue. (Job 5:21 NIV)
3. Spent their time in nothing ____, but either to tell, or to hear some new thing. (Acts 17:21)
4. For the ____ border, ye shall even have the great sea. (Num. 34:6)
5. An ark of bulrushes, and daubed it with ____. (Exod. 2:3)
6. A great star from heaven, burning as it were a ____. (Rev. 8:10)
7. Endanger.
8. God accepteth no man's ____. (Gal. 2:6)
9. The second death ____ no power over them. (Rev. 20:6 NIV)
10. They would have repented long ____ in sackcloth. (Matt. 11:21)
11. He lieth in wait secretly as a lion in his ____. (Ps. 10:9)
17. That which groweth of ____ own accord. (Lev. 25:5)
19. Noun suffix.
22. ____, which was the son of Seth. (Luke 3:38)
23. A ____ of him shall not be broken. (John 19:36)
24. Achaia was ready a ____ ago. (2 Cor. 9:2)
25. The name of the ____ is called Wormwood. (Rev. 8:11)
26. He ____ the chains apart and broke the irons. (Mark 5:4 NIV)
27. Reckon.
28. Maimed, or having a ____, or scurvy. (Lev. 22:22)
31. I will build myself a ____ with spacious rooms upstairs. (Jer. 22:14 GNB)
32. Five cubits also, ____ to the wing of the other cherub. (2 Chron. 3:12)
34. This world, according to the ____ of the power of air. (Eph. 2:2)

35. For (Spanish).
37. North Caucasian language.
38. The father of such as dwell in ____. (Gen. 4:20)
40. The love of many shall wax ____. (Matt. 24:12)
41. ____, lama sabachthani? (Mark 15:34)
42. His ____ drew the third part of the stars. (Rev. 12:4)
43. Paul stood in the midst of Mars' ____. (Acts 17:22)
44. Why did ____ remain in ships? (Judg. 5:17)
45. Copper is smelted from ____. (Job 28:2 NIV)
46. Yet in the loins of his father, when Melchisedec ____ him. (Heb. 7:10)

50

Across

1. The son of Nathan of Zobah, ____ the Gadite. (2 Sam. 23:36)
5. Abideth not in the doctrine of Christ, hath not ____. (2 John 9)
8. Oaks and poplars and ____, because the shadow thereof is good. (Hos. 4:13)
12. Adjective-forming suffix.
13. The wheat and the ____ were not smitten. (Exod. 9:32)
14. Rejoice ye in that day, and ____ for joy. (Luke 6:23)
15. ____ was tender eyed; but Rachel was beautiful. (Gen. 29:17)
16. The ____ favoured and leanfleshed kine. (Gen. 41:4)
17. Was in the ____ that is called Patmos. (Rev. 1:9)
18. Rejoice, thou ____ that bearest not. (Gal. 4:27)
20. Ye have ____ that the Lord is gracious. (1 Peter 2:3)
22. That we may obtain mercy, ____ find grace to help in time of need. (Heb. 4:16)
23. He . . . lifts the needy from the ____ heap. (1 Sam. 2:8 NIV)
24. (Fine linen ____ for the righteous acts.) (Rev. 19:8 NIV)
27. He who ____ the rod hates his son. (Prov. 13:24 NIV)
31. Head of Benjamin's clan.
32. Of ____, the family of the Erites. (Num. 26:16)
33. A ruler without good sense will be a cruel ____. (Prov. 28:16 GNB)
37. The Lord is very pitiful, and of ____ mercy. (James 5:11)
40. In all things ye are ____ superstitious. (Acts 17:22)
41. ____ no man any thing. (Rom. 13:8)
42. What causes ____ and quarrels among you? (James 4:1 NIV)
45. Removed the unnecessary.
49. Terror, consumption, and the burning ____. (Lev. 26:16)
50. Of Keros, the children of ____. (Neh. 7:47)
52. A ____ vision has been shown to me. (Isa. 21:2 NIV)
53. Horace or Thomas.

54. Do they not ____ that devise evil? (Prov. 14:22)
55. The ____ man which was healed held Peter and John. (Acts 3:11)
56. The iniquity of ____ house shall not be purged. (1 Sam. 3:14)
57. Be not, as the hypocrites, of a ____ countenance. (Matt. 6:16)
58. I will set my throne in ____. (Jer. 49:38)

Down

1. Onion starter.
2. Our ____ of activity among you will greatly expand. (2 Cor. 10:15 NIV)
3. Let us draw ____ with a true heart. (Heb. 10:22)
4. Shamma, and Shilshah, and ____, and Beera. (1 Chron. 7:37)
5. The mill as it ____ or music as it plays. (Eccles. 12:4 GNB)
6. My head with ____ thou didst not anoint. (Luke 7:46)
7. Greek letters.
8. Touched the bones of ____, he revived. (2 Kings 13:21)
9. Eat of it, neither shall ye touch it, ____ ye die. (Gen. 3:3)
10. Every ____ that openeth the womb shall be called holy to the Lord. (Luke 2:23)
11. Have they not ____? have they not divided the prey? (Judg. 5:30)
19. Overcometh, and keepeth my works unto the ____. (Rev. 2:26)
21. Shall play on the hole of the ____. (Isa. 11:8)
24. I ____ a queen, and am no widow. (Rev. 18:7)
25. The fiery trial which is to ____ you. (1 Peter 4:12)
26. The sun and the ____ were darkened. (Rev. 9:2)
28. Look not thou upon the wine when it is ____. (Prov. 23:31)
29. How long will it be ____ they believe? (Num. 14:11)
30. ____, we would see Jesus. (John 12:21)
34. We thought it good to be left at ____ alone. (1 Thess. 3:1)
35. The ship was caught, and could ____ bear up. (Acts 27:15)

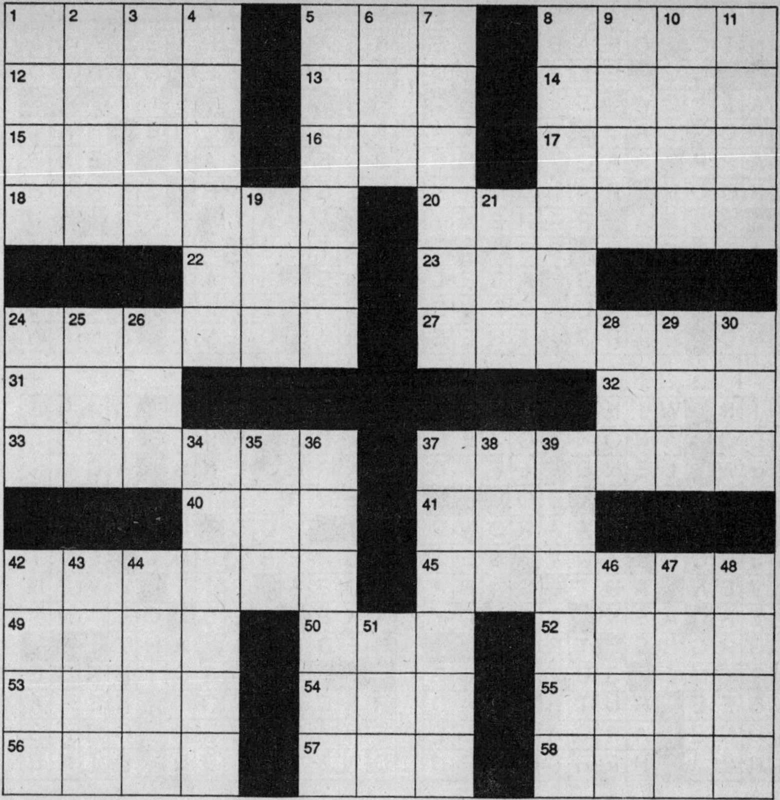

36. The Daughter of Jerusalem ____ her head as you flee. (Isa. 37:22 NIV)
37. In this was manifested the love of God ____ us. (1 John 4:9)
38. Cow or ____, ye shall not kill it and her young both in one day. (Lev. 22:28)
39. It is easier for a camel to go through the eye of a ____. (Mark 10:25)
42. Herod the tetrarch heard of the ____ of Jesus. (Matt. 14:1)
43. ____ the son of Nathan of Zobah. (2 Sam. 23:36)
44. Of ____, the family of the Gunites. (Num. 26:48)
46. In the sun ____ of Ahaz, ten degrees backward. (Isa. 38:8)
47. Woman's name.
48. Those members of the body, which we ____ less honorable. (1 Cor. 12:23 NASB)
51. ____ the son of Ikkesh the Tekoite. (1 Chron. 27:9)

1

```
A S A S   E D A R   L A W
H U N T   G A T E   A G E
I N T O   G R A B   S E E
      O G   E L E C T E D
H A L L O W   E L I
A D O   D A M   S T R A W
H A R P   S A G   Y O K E
A R D O N   R A M   M A N
      S E A   P A R E N T
P A T T E R N   D O
A R E   D O E S   A B E L
R A N   L E A D   S A V E
E N D   E R R S   T R E E
```

2

```
R I B   W I N E   C A S A
A D O   A N O N   O X E N
N E W   L E N D   L E W D
G A L I L E E   D O
      R E D   A A R O N S
H E R O D   A N Y   N E T
O V E N   A R T   S A R A
P E A   A S K   A N N O Y
E R R O R S   T R A
      M E   S U P P O S E
A G E E   R U T H   B A D
S U N G   A R O A   E V E
A R E A   H E R D   D E N
```

3

```
P A S S   R O E   S W A N
O B O E   E A R   C A R E
S E R E   P R E P A R E D
E Z E K I A S   A N
      A N Y   A T T E N D
T H I N K   O N E   L I E
H A N D   B A T   B O N E
A R C   M A R   C R I E D
T E H R A N   L E O
      A I   M A T T H E W
D O M I N I O N   H I D E
O N A N   D O E   E V E R
G I N S   E N S   R E N T
```

4

```
H E A R   S W I M   Y E A
E L S E   H A R E   E A R
R E A D   A R I D   A S A
D E S E R V E   D A R E D
      E Y E   E L I
F R A M E   O N E   H A I
L O S S   B A D   T E N T
Y E S   W A R   S E N D S
      M A T   B E N
H A T E S   R E A S O N S
E N E   H E A L   O P A L
I N A   E V I L   N E M O
R A M   D E N S   S N E W
```

5

```
F L A T   T A R   D A R E
R I D E   R U E   I D O L
E N A M   E N S   A D D I
T E M P T A T I O N
      L O D   D I A L E D
A G R E E   B U L   E V I
D O E S   P I E   E V E R
A R E   L L D   G L I N T
R E D S E A   A R T
      C O N S C I E N C E
R A C A   T O O   K E L A
E R A N   E R R   O R A S
D A R T   D E N   N I N E
```

6

```
L I E   A D A M   H A R A
E N D   D I M E   E N O S
A T E   O D O R   A D D S
H O N O R   S C A R
      W E T   Y I E L D S
S O U N D E D   D R E A M
A B C   N U N   V I E
L O A N S   G E N T I L E
A L L O W S   O U R
      R E N T   M Y S I A
C A L M   O R E B   A S P
A R E A   W E R E   S H E
R E E L   Y E A R   H I S
```

7

```
E L M S   F A D E   A L L
R E A L   O D E L   D O E
S A R A   R O V E   A N T
T H A N K S G I V I N G S
      G O O   L E D
W E B   R O T   N O B L E
A R E A   K O A   L A I N
S E L L S   I R A   R E D
      S A P   I S H
J E H O V A H S H A L O M
O N E   E L O I   R E B A
N O R   T E R N   E V I L
A S S   H A N G   M I L E
```

10

```
A R A B   A D A H   S E A
S O D A   R A G E   A I R
S P A R   A T E R   I R A
T E R R A C E   A D E N
      E R E   E L I
S C A N T   A V E N G E D
O A R   S S E   E A R
W R E A T H S   P E T T Y
      C O Y   B E L
W A N T   T E N D I N G
O N E   S A R A   E D E R
R O E   A L A S   R O B E
E N D   W E P T   S L O W
```

8

```
W A D E   T O P   P E R U
E L I M   W A R   A S A S
L I S P   E R A   S A T E
D E C I D E   I S S U E S
    I R O N   S E E
P A P E R   R E A D E S T
A W L   A I D   T H E
W E E P I N G   A S H E N
    A N T   T I K I
S T R I K E   O N I O N S
L A I N   S A W   E P E E
E L S E   U S E   R I A L
W E E D   P A R   S A R A
```

11

```
P A T H   A B E D   H A M
A R R O   S E A R   O L E
W E A R   H E R E   A S A
S A V I O U R   A A R O N
    E Z A R   A M I
V A L O R   A S S   C A W
O P E N   I N K   J O N A
W E D   P A Y   B E N D S
    H I M   F E A T
S T E A L   S E L L E R S
L O D   A C H E   O M A N
A R E   T R O D   U P T O
P E N   E Y E S   S T E W
```

9

```
O V E R   S S E   C H E W
H E R E   O I L   H E L I
A G A G   I R I   A R M S
D A N I E L   J A R O A H
    O N E   A R M
B A N N E D   H A S T E N
A G O         O R O
T E T H E R   B L A I N S
    O W E   R A N
A T O N E S   A N G E R S
L A N E   T O Y   E L A M
A R T S   E V E   L O N E
S P O T   D I D   S I T E
```

12

```
W I T H   A G E E   A S A
A R E A   R O L L   R A B
R A N G   A R I D   A R E
    A I   E T E R N A L
N E A R L Y   E R E
O D D   L E T   S A T A N
A D A H   T I N   R O D E
H O N O R   P O T   R A T
      M E L   W A T E R S
F O R E V E R   R I
I R I   I G A L   M E D E
L E D   L A C E   E V E N
E N E   E L A M   S E N D
```

13

A	S	S		P	A	C	E		S	A	I	L
R	A	T		E	R	A	N		I	S	L	E
A	R	E		R	O	L	E		M	A	L	E
B	A	P	T	I	S	M		D	O			
		H	O	E		M	O	N	T	H	S	
G	R	E	E	D		S	A	G		R	E	A
N	A	A	M		S	A	W		S	E	A	M
A	C	T		D	A	Y		W	H	E	R	E
W	A	S	T	E	D		A	R	E			
		O	N		P	R	O	M	I	S	E	
S	N	O	W		T	H	E	N		D	A	Y
H	E	W	N		H	U	N	G		E	W	E
E	W	E	S		E	T	A	S		A	N	D

16

A	R	C		O	N	E	S		S	E	T	S
S	A	H		R	I	S	K		C	A	R	E
P	H	I	L	I	P	P	I		O	R	E	N
	L	E	G		Y	E	A	R	N	E	D	
O	R	D	A	I	N		S	I	N			
W	A	R		N	O	T		N	E	C	K	S
E	P	E	E		D	E	N		D	A	N	E
D	E	N	S	E		N	U	N		L	E	E
		C	A	R		T	O	I	L	E	D	
T	R	E	A	T	E	D		I	R	I		
H	E	A	P		P	R	E	S	E	N	C	E
E	L	S	E		E	A	V	E		G	A	Y
E	Y	E	D		L	Y	E	S		S	T	E

14

H	A	S		D	E	S	K		S	L	A	T
U	S	E		E	L	O	I		H	E	R	O
T	H	E	S	T	E	R	N		O	V	E	R
		M	A	C	E	D	O	N	I	A	N	
A	L	B	E	I	T		R	I	E			
K	O	R	A	N		B	E	L		H	I	D
A	D	A	R		C	U	D		B	O	D	E
N	E	T		S	L	Y		H	O	R	O	N
		M	I	O		V	E	R	I	L	Y	
C	O	R	I	N	T	H	I	A	N			
A	B	E	L		H	A	S	T	E	N	E	D
L	O	N	E		E	S	T	E		O	W	E
L	E	T	S		S	T	A	D		T	E	N

15

F	A	N		S	P	A	N		H	A	T	E
L	A	O		I	L	S	E		I	R	A	D
A	R	A		N	U	I	T		R	A	R	E
G	E	H	E	N	N	A		B	A	B	E	L
		B	E	D		S	E	M				
R	E	F	E	R	E	N	C	E		C	A	R
A	G	A	R		R	E	A		T	O	R	E
N	O	R		W	E	A	T	H	E	R	E	D
		G	O	D		T	I	N				
A	A	R	O	N		R	E	S	T	I	N	G
C	L	O	D		M	A	R	S		L	E	E
R	E	E	L		A	G	E	E		A	X	E
E	A	S	Y		W	E	D	S		I	T	S

17

A	R	A	M		A	T	E		T	W	A	S
S	U	R	E		L	O	T		R	A	I	L
A	S	I	A		T	I	E		A	D	D	I
S	T	A	N	C	E		R	E	D	E	E	M
		E	A	R		N	O	E				
S	T	E	R	N		W	A	N	D	E	R	S
O	A	R		O	I	L		V	I	A		
P	R	E	S	E	N	T		S	T	E	E	P
		O	N	E		S	E	E				
B	U	I	L	D	S		A	T	T	E	S	T
E	L	S	E		I	N	N		H	A	H	A
C	A	L	M		D	I	D		E	V	E	R
A	M	E	N		E	L	Y		R	E	D	S

18

F	L	A	P		S	H	E		B	A	S	E
L	O	S	E		C	A	R		E	R	O	S
E	S	A	R		E	Y	E		W	A	I	T
A	S	S	I	G	N		C	R	A	D	L	E
		S	A	T		T	A	R				
L	I	G	H	T	S		S	M	E	L	L	S
I	R	I							O	I	L	
T	A	N	N	E	D		P	R	E	T	T	Y
		E	R	I		A	I	L				
T	A	V	E	R	N		R	E	D	E	E	M
O	B	E	D		N	O	T		E	L	S	E
N	A	I	L		E	W	E		R	I	P	S
I	D	L	E		R	E	D		S	A	Y	S

19

```
LORD . ARA . IDLE
AREO . RUN . SEAN
MEND . EGG . RAID
ENTRAP . LEARNS
. ONO . ERE . .
SCEPTRE . SLASH
MAR . TRA . SEE
ABRAM . ABRAHAM
. WAS . SOD . .
DONATE . ABODES
AVER . AWL . RIDE
READ . TOO . EVEN
ERRS . SEM . SAND
```

22

```
CAB . AGHA . WAST
AGO . TRAP . ISUI
MER . HEST . NILE
PERFECT . SENDS
. OENO . RIB . .
BOWLS . CURIOUS
OREL . DAN . BISE
ABDOMEN . ABNER
. WEN . TRET . .
BOAST . CHARMED
OUCH . DAUB . EVE
ISHI . AMMI . NEW
STEP . REBA . TRY
```

20

```
MASK . ALIT . SAG
ULAI . COLA . AGO
DAWN . HALLOWED
. GLAD . LINES .
GARDEN . BEL . .
AFOOT . HER . ADD
PALM . GAD . BLUE
ERE . SEM . ALONE
. SAT . SLOWED .
SHEER . OWLS . .
PARADISE . SODA
ARA . IDEA . ONAN
TEN . SEER . MEND
```

23

```
ARAM . ELAN . THE
NICE . LONE . HOR
EPHESIANS . EWE
TEETH . NOTED . .
. SIN . YEARNS
FAR . POT . DROOP
ANEW . DRY . ESAU
CAMEL . YEW . SHE
THERED . AHA . .
. MEDIA . ISSUE
WEB . GALATIANS
ARE . ENAN . DRIP
SIR . SASS . EASY
```

21

```
SAD . RAIL . SWAY
ONO . ARRA . HATE
ONESIMUS . USES
TARES . SEES . .
. TEN . ABHORS
ARA . DOG . BAMAH
MUCH . DAM . NERO
ASHUR . PAH . NEW
THESIN . NOE . .
. BEES . WROTE
ABBA . PHILEMON
LOAN . AONE . AND
LAND . LEND . RES
```

24

```
LEAH . GATE . LED
ASIA . AREA . USE
ISMS . RENT . KEN
NESTED . TIME . .
. ERE . SNOWIS
BEA . INK . GRADE
ARCH . SEM . ERLE
JACOB . YES . MEN
ANIMAL . SIN . .
. DENY . STEADY
EYE . IDEA . AGUE
WEN . SING . REEL
EAT . HADE . SELL
```

25

S	L	A	B		R	I	M		S	K	I	M
T	O	R	A		E	R	E		A	N	N	A
A	G	A	R		D	A	M		L	O	T	I
R	E	B	U	K	E		B	O	T	T	O	M
			C	O	E		E	W	E			
J	O	T	H	A	M		R	E	D	U	C	E
O	N	O							S	A	Y	
B	E	W	A	R	E		I	M	P	E	D	E
		W	A	S		N	O	R				
E	N	C	A	M	P		J	A	I	R	U	S
C	O	O	K		I	R	U		S	U	R	E
H	O	M	E		E	A	R		O	L	G	A
O	N	E	S		D	E	Y		N	E	E	R

28

S	P	A	T		W	E	B		S	A	L	E
L	A	S	H		A	W	E		E	R	I	N
A	G	E	E		S	E	L	E	C	T	E	D
Y	E	A	S	T		S	O	L	O			
			S	O	N		W	I	N	T	E	R
P	A	R	A	D	E	S		A	D	A	G	E
A	M	I	L		W	H	O		T	R	O	N
S	A	M	O	A		E	A	S	I	E	S	T
S	T	E	N	C	H		R	U	M			
			I	C	E	S		M	O	T	H	S
C	R	E	A	T	I	O	N		T	H	A	T
E	A	R	N		R	O	E		H	E	R	A
A	N	I	S		S	T	R		Y	E	A	R

26

A	L	A	S		S	P	E	D		B	A	T
D	I	S	H		A	R	E	A		A	G	E
O	P	P	O	R	T	U	N	I	T	I	E	S
		W	A	I	T		N	O	T	E	S	
A	S	S	I	G	N		A	T	E			
S	H	I	N	E		C	R	Y		R	A	B
P	O	N	G		G	A	T		B	A	T	E
S	A	G		D	O	R		S	L	I	M	E
		D	O	G		T	I	E	D	O	N	
A	G	R	E	E		A	R	T	S			
T	R	A	N	S	G	R	E	S	S	I	O	N
E	A	T		N	A	M	E		E	R	N	E
R	Y	E		T	O	S	S		D	I	E	T

29

M	O	A	B		A	S	A		V	E	N	T
A	B	L	E		R	E	D		I	L	A	I
R	E	S	E	N	T	E	D		S	E	M	E
A	D	O	R	E		R	E	V	I	V	E	D
		I	R	A		R	A	T	E			
J	O	B		O	W	E		T	E	N	T	H
A	I	L	S		L	A	D		D	A	R	E
S	L	E	E	T		R	A	T		S	Y	N
		S	T	O	P		M	O	W			
I	N	S	T	E	A	D		S	A	M	O	A
T	O	I	L		R	O	A	S	T	I	N	G
A	N	N	E		A	M	I		E	N	C	E
L	E	G	S		H	E	R		R	E	E	D

27

A	S	H		S	T	A	R		A	L	S	O
I	R	U		C	A	G	E		L	I	E	N
R	O	S		O	B	E	D	I	E	N	C	E
		B	E	L	L	S		T	R	E	T	S
G	R	A	N	D	E		S	E	T			
L	A	N	D	S		H	A	M		P	O	T
A	I	D	S		T	O	W		S	A	R	A
D	D	S		L	I	P		P	E	T	E	R
		A	I	N		P	R	A	I	S	E	
A	L	A	R	M		A	R	I	S	E		
D	E	C	R	E	A	S	E	D		N	O	E
D	U	R	A		R	A	S	E		C	A	N
S	K	E	Y		A	S	S	S		E	R	E

30

R	A	F	T		H	A	H	A		L	O	D
A	D	A	H		O	B	O	L		O	N	E
M	O	T	E		W	E	S	T		I	C	E
		H	I	E		L	E	A	R	N	E	D
E	N	E	R	G	Y		A	R	A			
D	A	R		G	E	T		S	I	F	T	S
G	I	E	R		T	O	O		L	A	A	P
E	L	D	E	R		W	I	T		I	R	I
		A	I	A		L	I	S	T	E	N	
T	H	I	R	S	T	S		E	T	H		
A	I	R		E	T	A	M		A	F	A	R
I	R	A		T	A	L	E		R	U	L	E
L	E	D		H	I	E	L		S	L	I	D

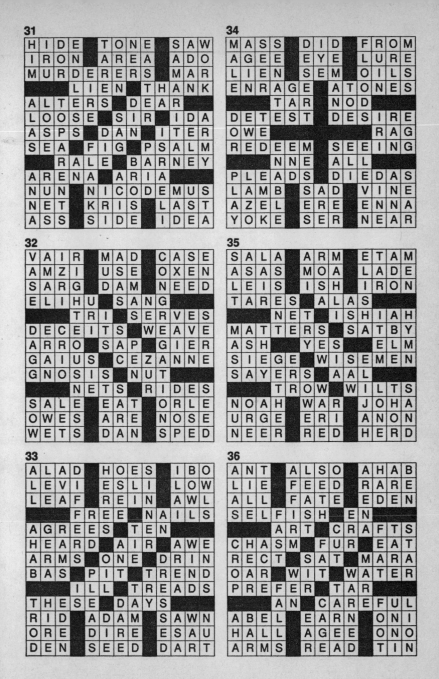

31

H	I	D	E		T	O	N	E		S	A	W
I	R	O	N		A	R	E	A		A	D	O
M	U	R	D	E	R	E	R	S		M	A	R
		L	I	E	N		T	H	A	N	K	
A	L	T	E	R	S		D	E	A	R		
L	O	O	S	E		S	I	R		I	D	A
A	S	P	S		D	A	N		I	T	E	R
S	E	A		F	I	G		P	S	A	L	M
	R	A	L	E		B	A	R	N	E	Y	
A	R	E	N	A		A	R	I	A			
N	U	N		N	I	C	O	D	E	M	U	S
N	E	T		K	R	I	S		L	A	S	T
A	S	S		S	I	D	E		I	D	E	A

34

M	A	S	S		D	I	D		F	R	O	M
A	G	E	E		E	Y	E		L	U	R	E
L	I	E	N		S	E	M		O	I	L	S
E	N	R	A	G	E		A	T	O	N	E	S
			T	A	R		N	O	D			
D	E	T	E	S	T		D	E	S	I	R	E
O	W	E							R	A	G	
R	E	D	E	E	M		S	E	E	I	N	G
		N	N	E		A	L	L				
P	L	E	A	D	S		D	I	E	D	A	S
L	A	M	B		S	A	D		V	I	N	E
A	Z	E	L		E	R	E		E	N	N	A
Y	O	K	E		S	E	R		N	E	A	R

32

V	A	I	R		M	A	D		C	A	S	E
A	M	Z	I		U	S	E		O	X	E	N
S	A	R	G		D	A	M		N	E	E	D
E	L	I	H	U		S	A	N	G			
			T	R	I		S	E	R	V	E	S
D	E	C	E	I	T	S		W	E	A	V	E
A	R	R	O		S	A	P		G	I	E	R
G	A	I	U	S		C	E	Z	A	N	N	E
G	N	O	S	I	S		N	U	T			
			N	E	T	S		R	I	D	E	S
S	A	L	E		E	A	T		O	R	L	E
O	W	E	S		A	R	E		N	O	S	E
W	E	T	S		D	A	N		S	P	E	D

35

S	A	L	A		A	R	M		E	T	A	M
A	S	A	S		M	O	A		L	A	D	E
L	E	I	S		I	S	H		I	R	O	N
T	A	R	E	S		A	L	A	S			
			N	E	T		I	S	H	I	A	H
M	A	T	T	E	R	S		S	A	T	B	Y
A	S	H		Y	E	S			E	L	M	
S	I	E	G	E		W	I	S	E	M	E	N
S	A	Y	E	R	S		A	A	L			
			T	R	O	W		W	I	L	T	S
N	O	A	H		W	A	R		J	O	H	A
U	R	G	E		E	R	I		A	N	O	N
N	E	E	R		R	E	D		H	E	R	D

33

A	L	A	D		H	O	E	S		I	B	O
L	E	V	I		E	S	L	I		L	O	W
L	E	A	F		R	E	I	N		A	W	L
			F	R	E	E		N	A	I	L	S
A	G	R	E	E	S		T	E	N			
H	E	A	R	D		A	I	R		A	W	E
A	R	M	S		O	N	E		D	R	I	N
B	A	S		P	I	T		T	R	E	N	D
			I	L	L		T	R	E	A	D	S
T	H	E	S	E		D	A	Y	S			
R	I	D		A	D	A	M		S	A	W	N
O	R	E		D	I	R	E		E	S	A	U
D	E	N		S	E	E	D		D	A	R	T

36

A	N	T		A	L	S	O		A	H	A	B
L	I	E		F	E	E	D		R	A	R	E
A	L	L		F	A	T	E		E	D	E	N
S	E	L	F	I	S	H		E	N			
			A	R	T		C	R	A	F	T	S
C	H	A	S	M		F	U	R		E	A	T
R	E	C	T		S	A	T		M	A	R	A
O	A	R		W	I	T		W	A	T	E	R
P	R	E	F	E	R		T	A	R			
			A	N		C	A	R	E	F	U	L
A	B	E	L		E	A	R	N		O	N	I
H	A	L	L		A	G	E	E		O	N	O
A	R	M	S		R	E	A	D		T	I	N

37

H	A	S		A	N	E	W		A	L	A	S
O	W	E		L	A	M	A		S	A	G	E
R	E	M	E	M	B	E	R		I	D	E	A
		T	O	A		R	E	D	E	E	M	
A	A	R	O	N	S		I	R	E			
B	L	I	N	D		W	O	E		A	D	D
L	O	S	S		D	O	R		T	R	I	O
E	W	E		O	W	N		L	E	A	V	E
		A	R	E		P	O	N	D	E	R	
C	A	R	M	E	L		A	N	T			
A	S	E	A		L	A	U	G	H	T	E	R
M	I	S	S		E	L	S	E		I	R	A
E	A	T	S		D	I	E	D		P	I	N

40

L	I	M	E		A	H	A	B		H	E	W
A	R	E	A		S	A	L	E		E	V	E
W	I	N	G		P	L	O	T		R	E	D
		E	N		L	E	T	T	E	R	S	
F	E	A	R	E	D		S	E	E			
E	D	M		T	O	W		R	E	S	T	S
L	A	M	A		E	A	R		M	I	R	E
T	R	I	M	S		G	A	T		N	U	N
		O	I	L		M	I	S	S	E	D	
P	L	A	S	T	E	R		N	O			
O	A	R		N	A	I	A		U	R	G	E
O	N	I		A	V	E	N		L	E	E	S
L	E	D		H	E	R	D		S	A	M	E

38

S	O	D	A		O	A	K	S		B	A	R
E	D	O	M		W	I	N	E		L	I	E
C	O	M	M	A	N	D	E	R		E	N	D
T	R	O	A	S		S	L	I	P	S		
		H	E	N		L	E	A	S	E	S	
O	L	D		R	U	N		S	T	I	L	L
D	E	E	M		N	O	R		A	N	O	A
D	A	T	E	S		T	O	I		G	I	P
S	H	E	E	T	S		I	C	E			
		S	T	A	T	E		A	L	A	M	E
W	O	T		B	E	T	H	L	E	H	E	M
E	W	E		L	E	T	E		A	I	D	E
B	E	D		E	D	E	R		D	O	E	R

41

C	A	R		T	R	E	E		S	A	M	E
O	N	I		H	E	A	R		I	G	A	L
O	N	O		R	A	S	E		M	E	D	I
L	A	T	T	I	C	E		L	O			
		I	C	H		R	E	N	D	E	R	
F	L	A	M	E		S	A	G		R	I	E
L	U	R	E		G	O	T		E	A	R	N
A	T	E		T	O	P		C	A	G	E	D
T	E	A	S	E	D		A	R	T			
		I	N		E	P	I	S	T	L	E	
A	K	A	N		A	D	A	M		R	I	D
S	O	N	G		H	A	R	E		I	C	E
P	A	Y	S		A	R	T	S		P	E	N

39

A	R	A	B		T	H	E		D	I	B	S
D	U	R	A		R	A	W		E	S	E	K
A	D	E	N		E	N	E		G	U	N	I
M	E	A	N	I	N	G		O	R	I	O	N
		E	N	D		O	N	E				
L	E	A	R	N		F	R	I	E	N	D	S
I	R	I		R	O	E		O	N	O		
D	E	L	I	V	E	R		B	R	E	A	D
		S	A	D		F	E	E				
D	E	A	L	T		E	L	E	A	S	A	H
I	M	N	A		A	D	O		P	A	L	E
A	M	O	N		S	E	A		E	R	A	N
L	A	N	D		A	N	T		D	A	R	A

42

E	G	G	S		L	E	D		H	A	S	H
S	O	A	P		E	R	R		A	R	E	A
E	D	D	O		A	M	I		R	E	A	D
		I	C	H	A	B	O	D				
S	T	A	L	E			N	E	S	T	S	
T	A	R		L	O	S	T		N	A	I	L
A	B	I		L	A	H	A	I		I	D	A
F	L	O	G		R	E	I	N		N	A	V
F	E	T	I	D			T	I	T	L	E	
		L	O	R	D	G	O	D				
R	A	N	G		I	R	A		O	N	E	S
I	D	E	A		S	A	T		L	O	V	E
B	O	W	L		E	W	E		S	T	E	W

43

```
A S S   T I R E   S P E D
L E O   A N A T   H O R I
A N D   B E T H L E H E M
S T A B L E S   O O
      R E D   B A L A A M
S A R A S   S O N   D U E
P R A Y   D A Y   M A L A
E R I   L I P   H A M A N
W A N T E D   O A R
      R A   A B R A H A M
J E R U S A L E M   A R E
O N E S   E S S E   R A N
B E S T   T O E D   A D D
```

46

```
R O A R   B A R   S A C K
O G R E   E W E   T R U E
L E A F   L E T   R E S T
L E M U E L   U R I A H S
      S A Y   R O D
P A P E R   S N E E Z E D
A R E   T I S   E R I
L A N T E R N   T H R E E
      A T E   H O E
E L I S H A   A P R O N S
L A D S   D I M   O B I L
A D O E   E R A   D A T E
H E L L   R A N   S L O W
```

44

```
E K E R   A S H   T H I S
L I V E   I T A   R O T A
I D E A   L E G   O P E N
      C O M M A N D I N G
S E T T L E   R E D
E R R   E N D   T E E T H
T O U R   T I S   N A R Y
A S E E R   E A T   S E M
      P A S   B I T T E N
D O R E M E M B E R
A M E N   M O A   U S E S
T E N T   E S T   S H O E
A R T S   I S H   T E S T
```

47

```
D R A W   S E E D   R I D
E I R E   E L S E   E R E
C E A S E L E S S   M A N
      T A L E   E N E M Y
P A P E R S   D R U M
A D O R N   W E T   B U D
L E O N   S I N   W E R E
E R R   R U N   M E R G E
      L I E N   C E A S E D
A R E N A   B O W L
W I N   C H R I S T I A N
A D D   T O O N   H O L E
Y E S   S E W S   Y U L E
```

45

```
H A R M   W A W   E B A L
E S A U   E L I   L A C E
M A N S   I S T   E A R S
      C H R O N I C L E S
S O I L E D   E A T
A B N E R   I S M   S A W
L E T S   W A S   R I P E
A D O   T E N   T A R E S
      E H I   V O W E S T
B R I D E G R O O M
R U N G   H A M   E A T S
E T R E   T R I   A S I A
R H O S   Y E T   T H E Y
```

48

```
B A R B   R E A D   D A N
O B O E   A A R E   E R E
A L O G   I T E M   C A R
R E F O R M   N O T E
      T I E   A N O I N T
W A S   E N D   S E V E R
A C H E   T I N   S E R A
D R I L L   G A S   R I P
S E E S A W   T I P
      L E A H   U R I A H S
F E D   D O O R   P R A E
O W E   A S I A   E A R N
R E D   H E L L   S H E D
```

49

S	L	E	W		S	L	I	P		H	A	D
P	A	L	E		L	A	M	E		A	G	E
A	S	S	S		I	M	P	R	I	S	O	N
T	H	E	T	E	M	P	E	S	T			
			E	N	E		R	O	S	E	B	Y
S	T	A	R	T		W	I	N		N	O	E
T	O	R	N		M	E	L		J	O	N	A
A	R	E		P	A	N		P	O	S	E	R
R	E	T	U	R	N		T	O	I			
		D	I	S	C	E	R	N	E	T	H	
D	O	M	I	N	I	O	N		I	L	A	I
A	R	E		C	O	L	T		N	O	I	L
N	E	T		E	N	D	S		G	I	L	L

50

B	A	N	I		G	O	D		E	L	M	S
U	R	E	T		R	I	E		L	E	A	P
L	E	A	H		I	L	L		I	S	L	E
B	A	R	R	E	N		T	A	S	T	E	D
			A	N	D		A	S	H			
S	T	A	N	D	S		S	P	A	R	E	S
I	R	I							E	R	I	
T	Y	R	A	N	T		T	E	N	D	E	R
			T	O	O		O	W	E			
F	I	G	H	T	S		W	E	E	D	E	D
A	G	U	E		S	I	A		D	I	R	E
M	A	N	N		E	R	R		L	A	M	E
E	L	I	S		S	A	D		E	L	A	M